Dionne Pylpets Ra

ONCE UPON A DREAM

A Way With Words

Edited By Warren Arthur

First published in Great Britain in 2017 by:

Young Writers
Remus House
Coltsfoot Drive
Peterborough
PE2 9BF
Telephone: 01733 890066
Website: www.youngwriters.co.uk

All Rights Reserved
Book Design by Spencer Hart
© Copyright Contributors 2017
SB ISBN 978-1-78820-290-9
Printed and bound in the UK by BookPrintingUK
Website: www.bookprintinguk.com
YB0333VZ

FOREWORD

Welcome Reader, to 'Once Upon A Dream – A Way With Words'.

Do you dare to dream?

For Young Writers' latest poetry competition, we asked our writers to dig deep into their imagination and create a poem that paints a picture of what they dream of.

The result is this collection of fantastic poetic verse that covers a whole host of different topics. Snuggle up all comfy and let your mind fly away with the fairies to explore the sweet joy of candy lands, join in with a game of fantasy football, or you may even catch a glimpse of a unicorn or another mythical creature. This collection has a poem to suit everyone.

Whereas the majority of our writers chose to stick to a free verse style, others gave themselves the challenge of other techniques such as acrostics and rhyming couplets.

There was a great response to this competition which is always nice to see, and the standard of entries was excellent. Therefore I'd like to say congratulations to the winner in this book, Darshan Sakthivel, for their amazing poem, and a big thank you to everyone else who entered.

Warren Arthur

CONTENTS

Winner:

Darshan Sakthivel (10) - Reddiford School, Pinner — 1

Barnfield Primary School, Burnt Oak

Arfaan Fazli (8)	2
Duha Yasser (8)	3
Daniel Olayiwole (8)	4
Khanak Khedkar (8)	5
David Olayiwole (8)	6
Andy Mirauta (7)	7
Rukiya Omar (8)	8
Dawid Orzel (8)	9
Alexandra Suman (7)	10
Nooh Nasir (8)	11
George Savva (8)	12
Jonelle Forbes (8)	13

Elizabeth College Junior School - Beechwood, St. Peter Port

George Corfield (8)	14
Emily Kate Northmore (10)	15
Christina Kennedy (10)	16
William James Hemans (9)	17
Eleanor Julia Whittaker (10)	18
Jago Holden (9)	20
Abigail Boyle (9)	21
Charlie Forshaw	22
Felix Thomas Jack Addenbrooke (9)	24
Seve Jack Falla (9)	25
Casper Le Ray	26
Ralph Humphries (8)	27

George Louis Le Roux (11)	28
Giulia Rihoy (9)	29
Rory Clarke (9)	30
Will Godfrey (9)	31
William Fysh (10)	32
Declan Andrew Crowther-Martel (9)	33
Jack Becker (10)	34
Alexa Annan (9)	35
Grace Clark (9)	36
Jack Gilbey (8)	37
Jack Meerveld (10)	38
Rupert Wilson (9)	39
Sam Romer (10)	40
Yannick Carpentier	41
Hugo Allen (8)	42
Jacky Marquis (9)	43
Oliver Bloor (9)	44
Sam Savory (9)	45
Will Horsbrugh-Porter (11)	46
Toby James McIntosh (9)	47
Charlie Reuben Tourtel (9)	48
Joe James (9)	49
Hugo Le Clerc	50
Yannick Gaudion (9)	51
Henry George Swanson (11)	52
George Peter Harris (10)	53

Parkland Junior School, Eastbourne

Alexander Herbert (10)	54
Izzie Gray (9)	55
Macie Smith (11)	56
Isabella Parmley (8)	57
Millie Barker (11)	58

Max Perry (8)	59
Holly (11) & Emma Furminger	60
Chloe Haizelden (10)	61
Jamie-Leigh Barnaville-Gibbs (11)	62
Cem Ali Çetin (10)	63
Josh Young (8)	64
Fraser Robert Mechan (10)	65
Leon Wilkinson (9)	66
Alfie William Young (10)	67
Rhys Binks (11)	68
Cerys Andrews (9)	69
Alex Andrew Modestou (8)	70
Angel Leigh Masters (10)	71
Will Smith (7)	72
Bailey Ashdown (10)	73
Noah Impey (11)	74
James Snashall (8)	75
Hebe Warren (10)	76
Kieran Hayward (8)	77
Django Swanmens	78
Amelia Bernard (9)	79
Ted Brickley (9)	80
Rory Arbenz (9)	81
Grace Bredemeier-Maher (8)	82
Thomas Elliott (9)	83
Zak Adams (9)	84
Kacie-Leigh Lambert (8)	85
Dylan White (9)	86
Phoenix Ana Parker	87
Ella Perry (10)	88
Zach Thomas (10)	89
Finley Goldsmith (8)	90
Aiden Barnaville-Gibbs (7)	91
Archie George Taylor (8)	92
Tom Nerhati (10)	93
Harry Jupp (8)	94
Oscar Lindfield (10)	95
Nomi Alicia Oakley (9)	96
Grace Kelly (8)	97
Jasmine Jakeman (8)	98
Cara Lewis (8)	99
Rhyley Willott (8)	100

Donte Adams (7)	101
Ime Emerald Janine Cox (8)	102
Max Theo Nightingale (10)	103
Max Ryan Oliver Gilbert (8)	104
Liam Delacy (10)	105
Jamie Keira Da Silva (10)	106
Ava Belle Woodrow (8)	107
Stanley Forder (8)	108
Josh Fox (7)	109
Curtis John Bint (10)	110
Ben Wilkinson (10)	111
Ella Waters (10)	112
Lucas Leonard Brown (8)	113

Portesham CE Primary School, Portesham

Jessica Steele (9)	114
Riffe Bradley (9)	115
Evie Bull (9)	116
Florence Farnham (8)	117
Charlotte Burgess (9)	118
Sulis Baird (9)	119
Gracie Summers (9)	120
Trinity McCann (9)	121
Sullie Yelland (9)	122
Daisy McCarthy (8)	123
Jake Stone (9)	124
Evie Prior (8)	125
Lexie Garland (7)	126
Megan Burgess (9)	127
Imogen Lilly Baber (9)	128
Ben Spencer-Veale (7)	129
Frank McCarthy (8)	130

Reddiford School, Pinner

Khush P Patel (11)	131
Ria Shah (11)	132
Caylan Zakharia	135
Vedika Rakesh Bhopatrao (11)	136
Eliza Mukhtar (11)	138
Aanya Dave	140
Riyah Solomons	142

Rhea Patel	144
Zaina Rasiah	146
Tia Desai (11)	147
Shaina Vadher (10)	148
Anya Vidyadhar (9)	149
Aaditya Anant Bhandarkar (10)	150
Zahra Elisa Iqbal (10)	151
Milen Pattni (10)	152
Lumanti Bajracharya (11)	153
Mili Shah (9)	154
Vernilan Vishnukumar (11)	155
Furqan Qadir	156
Alveena Dudhia (8)	157
James Gibbs	158
Anushka Srisuthan	159
Matthew Dancer (8)	160
Anusha Choubina (11)	161
Tomisin Esther Shitta-Bey (10)	162
Joshua Griffith (8)	163
Anjali Kylahsum (9)	164
Swastha Shankar (11)	165
Dylan Kankeyan Devabala (9)	166
Rihanna Radia (11)	167
Karina Desai (8)	168
Roshan Arora	169
Shreya Ashish Patel (10)	170
Avi Juneja (10)	171
Amey Gupta (10)	172
Harini Thirupaharan (10)	173
Georgia Moore (8)	174
Ashna Jitesh Halai	175
Shayam Jayesh Patel (9)	176
Harshita Sinhu (9)	177
Tiya Roma Patel (9)	178
Arnav Dubey	179
Krish Naik (8)	180
Anay Vaghela-Shah (10)	181
Dilan Amin (9)	182
Pradyun Sushena (9)	183
Samuel Rao Yarasani	184
Syun Patel	185
Dylan Patel	186
Ravi Karan Shah	187

Kareena Ahluwalia (9)	188
Ashvika Kotha	189
Rohan Parmar (10)	190
Zak Kupfer (9)	191
Boluwatife Anidugbe (8)	192

Slinfold CE Primary School, Slinfold

Greta Pitts (11)	193
Ryan McWatt (11)	194

St Philip's Catholic Primary School, Arundel

Brian Delali Tsikata (8)	196
Claude Young (8)	198
Autumn Sleven (7)	199

Yeading Junior School, Hayes

Ammarah Ahmed (10)	200
Dionne Pylypets Rabi (10)	202
Alia Ali	203
Leo Ojara (10)	204
Tanisha Kaur (10)	205
Roble Warsame (10)	206
Eliora Efrem (10)	207
Harmanpreet Chahal (10)	208
Satwinder Kaur Sandhu (10)	209
Layane Ali (9)	210
Vaughan Kirubakar (10)	211

THE POEMS

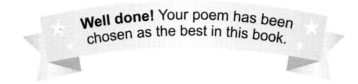

Once Upon An Icy Dream

Once upon a dream,
I saw an icy land,
It was a wonderful sight,
It had lots of flavour; never bland.

Swiftly, the blizzard stretched its icy legs
From out of the hollow night,
Stripping the world of all her scarlet pomp
And muffling her in white.

The snow blowing gently across my face,
Like tiny particles of sand.
The plants are covered full in white
And there the snow stands.

In inky curve, along the drifted snow
The sluggish river rolled.
A numb, black snake caught lingering in the sun
By autumn's sudden cold.

Darshan Sakthivel (10)
Reddiford School, Pinner

A Dream Which You'll Never Forget

O nce I woke and knew what to do.
N ow I can write a poem, woo hoo!
C ats or rats or bats or anything.
E veryone told me to say, 'Moo moo.'

U pon every person, they have different dreams.
P eople have different opinions.
O h can't you just dream of Spider-Man?
N o one dreams of Minions.

A dream is a dream, so we must keep on going, we can't just stop!

D reams come true or they may not.
R unning wild in your dreams never stop.
E veryone, they really love you.
A little boy just said to me, 'Stop!'
M um just said, 'This is bedtime!'

Arfaan Fazli (8)
Barnfield Primary School, Burnt Oak

Once Upon A Dream - A Way With Words

The Flying Unicorn And The Bird

U nicorns are flying, what should we do?

N o way to get them, ahhh, get them down!

I n a little unicorn cage, trying to get out!

C ome with me unicorn, you mustn't escape

O r I will get cross with you little unicorn!

R ight, come with me to take you to a unicorn park.

N ow you have got to behave and no flying.

B ye now, practise your flying.

I n you come to our little, teeny-tiny house.

R un and get that worm and eat it or you will starve.

D own you come, no we are not scared, we are above our goal.

Duha Yasser (8)
Barnfield Primary School, Burnt Oak

Humans

Humans, they can do lots
of things, like paying
bills and climbing hills.

But humans can be heinous,
like the ones who burn you
with something hot, like
a flaming pot.

And some humans are nice, like the ones
who play games with you,
like roll the dice.

But in my dream there were no humans
at all, you couldn't even
share a rubber ball.

There were also no
animals, like the ones who
roar or the ones who
soar.

Daniel Olayiwole (8)
Barnfield Primary School, Burnt Oak

My Royal Dream

R obo is my little brother that sleeps with me.

O h boy, I take him to a palace of the prince and princess, as royal as can be.

Y eah! What is that on my head? Crown! Is this what I can see?

A mazing, long, pink dress with long running veil.

L uxury train to take me from my room to a room full of toys and sweets.

T apping on the door was my family.

Y elled and screamed and found myself on the floor.

Khanak Khedkar (8)
Barnfield Primary School, Burnt Oak

Untitled

There is a clown trying to kill me with a spoon.
Run, run before he gets you, but should you?
Don't poo because he'll stab you when you're on the loo.

Get a giant water gun and shoot him with it.
Run, run, he will get you!
Or should I be running?

Wait... I live in a giant potato!
Let me pinch myself.
It's all a dream!
That explains why someone bathed with whipped cream!

David Olayiwole (8)
Barnfield Primary School, Burnt Oak

Writer Of The Poem

The writer of this poem might die
He doesn't like bread, that is pie.
So here's a fact that you should know,
The writer of the poem is strong and low.

So here's a special secret,
He always likes to write on leaflets.
This is how the poem begins,
The writer lives in Holiday Inns.

The writer is smart,
So he improved his art.
The writer likes to run,
So this is so fun.

Andy Mirauta (7)
Barnfield Primary School, Burnt Oak

A Great Dream Adventure!

Once upon a dream, there was this girl
who was made out of steam
and was in a forest that was beautiful anyway.
But still, it was a beautiful day.
But one day she disappeared
and she was sleeping right next to a dragon.
All I can see is smoke.
Oh, I hope this is a joke.
I just can't stand this any more.
Then steam was everywhere.
Then, I realised I was having a dream.
Luckily, I was safe.

Rukiya Omar (8)
Barnfield Primary School, Burnt Oak

I Had A Nightmare

I had a nightmare last night,
Which gave me a fright,
Of monsters chasing me
And a big, fat, red bee.

I had a nightmare last night,
Which gave me a fright,
Of this scary wizard
And a toothless, stinky, old lizard.

I had a nightmare last night,
Which gave me a fright,
Of humans eating cars
And me flying with an alien to Mars.

Dawid Orzel (8)
Barnfield Primary School, Burnt Oak

Magic Life Dream

Unicorns, look at their tails.
It's bigger than a snail, it's amazing.
There's even horses.
I'm in a fright,
Oh no, it's night.
Maybe I'll close my eyes.
Wow, am I at home?
I need to comb my hair,
It's ruining my bed.
I'd better be careful where I sleep.

That was an amazing dream!

Alexandra Suman (7)
Barnfield Primary School, Burnt Oak

The Dreams Of Football

In the world of enjoyment
Football lifts the air.
The skills are always flamboyant,
Both the sides say their prayer.

The team attacks, the fans are still,
Neymar tearing through the defence.
The fans chant through, what a thrill!
The pressure is immense.

Nooh Nasir (8)
Barnfield Primary School, Burnt Oak

Dinosaurs

D anger, danger, look!
I am not scared.
N o, no, no don't eat me.
O h how, they are so big.
S ee them run
A nd stomp around.
U nderneath the rocks I hide.
R oaring loudly everywhere.
S sh, the dinosaurs are coming!

George Savva (8)
Barnfield Primary School, Burnt Oak

Teachers Do Crazy Stuff!

Teachers are tall.
Teachers are small.
Teachers are smart
but work crazy!

Some teachers have fun.
Some teachers have none.
Some teachers have one.
Some teachers have none.

Jonelle Forbes (8)
Barnfield Primary School, Burnt Oak

Candy Land

There I lay in the darkness of night in my bed,
When suddenly a scene occurred deep in my head.
A goblin was holding a big hot spoon.
And the bad guys were locked up in jails like baboons.
A zing and zoom.
There was some ice cream.
My eyes grew heavier and further I did dream.
The roaring dragons then came into my dream, eating flakes.
And devils grew calm and dropped their forked rakes.
Dracula didn't drink blood any more
Instead he drank strawberry juice galore.
Suddenly, a monster with orange fur
Started to come over to have custard curd.
Like nothing before, I was walking along the path.
When I saw a giant taking a bath.
I said, 'Hello,' and he replied back
'Hello there, my name's Jack.'
A roll of mints came rushing down the hill.
I started to run but I could do nothing still.
I opened my eyes and I was in my room.
And there stood my mother holding a broom.

George Corfield (8)
Elizabeth College Junior School - Beechwood, St. Peter Port

A Shiny-Like Dream

As we entered the rocky crystal cave
all of a sudden I felt a wave
out of all the beauty in each little gem
I really loved the sight of them.

But down in a corner was a wall of stone.
I could see it was hollow so I whacked it with a bone
There was a crash and a thud, then down came the
wall
I caught a glimpse of a waterfall.

I saw animals and plants with a gem-like touch
My friend Lily and I loved it very much.

My favourite animal had shiny white fur
and dazzling gems, most of them silver.
It was strong and brave but friendly and fair
Why, I am talking about the polar bear.

This paradise was a wonderful place to be
with lots to do and lots to see
With its animal, gem and plant themes
But then I woke up, it was only one of my dreams!

Emily Kate Northmore (10)
Elizabeth College Junior School - Beechwood, St. Peter Port

Off To Dreamland

Late one evening when the stars were bright
And the moon poured down its silvery light,
I fell asleep and was swept far away
To a beautiful land where night looks like day!

It was a lovely old land where unicorns dance
And dinosaurs joust carrying a bright purple lance,
Where crocodiles frown and don't gnash their teeth
Where Excalibur hangs in its glittering sheath.

I stood on a path and looked round the bend
The sight was more than I could comprehend!
For there stood a chick making friends with a fox
Then they snuggled together on a pile of warm rocks.

Then up and away, away I did fly
Looking out of the window at the six o' clock sky
I was back in my bedroom and suddenly then
I wondered if I'd go to Dreamland again.

Christina Kennedy (10)
Elizabeth College Junior School - Beechwood, St. Peter Port

The Time Machine

I was standing there waiting for the bus.
To go to school, nay, nay, nay!
Another boring day at school!

At playtime there was a man saying,
'Come,' so I ran over the fence.
The teacher rang the police.
They came running after me, I ran down the alley.

Then appeared a time machine.
I set the clock five minutes, back...
And I froze the world.
I could do anything! I could blow up the school
And have hundreds of days off from school,
But I would never tell anyone about this.

It was pure evil, but I didn't care!
It turned out to be that the teacher was asking me
maths questions!
I was daydreaming!

William James Hemans (9)
Elizabeth College Junior School - Beechwood, St. Peter Port

My Crazy Dream!

The Queen
Was having a heck
Of a good time on the trampoline
While a teen
Was partying with a sardine.

There was a fairy
Flying with a canary
Which was rather hairy
Orangutans were going crazy
And the sloths were being super lazy.

I had a drink
That was called Tiddly Wink
It did stink
But it was really pink
In one blink
I was flying with Prince Humperdinck.

Splash! Crash!
I was in a mishmash
I looked like trash
But all of a sudden, I was in a dash
Thought I was as fast as flash.

I didn't seem
To realise this was a dream
Till I had another dream
with the theme...
Of ice cream!

Eleanor Julia Whittaker (10)

Elizabeth College Junior School - Beechwood, St. Peter Port

Imagination Land

I n the land of dreams there is a place
M atching the size of a sugar lace
A t that place in the sky
G rab some dust to make you fly
I n that land far, far away,
N on-stop partying all day
A t that point I heard my friend
T he dream is coming to an end
I now need to go back to bed
O r tomorrow I'll feel like a dead head
N ow it's time to go.

L oudly I hear a rumble from my belly
A t this moment it looks just like jelly
N ow I just want to cry and weep,
D on't worry, I'm just going back to sleep.

Jago Holden (9)
Elizabeth College Junior School - Beechwood, St. Peter Port

The Ghost Ship

As Sophie lay her golden locks
Upon her soft bed
The moon began to rise
As the sun settled its head.

Two emerald-green eyes closed tight
Her mind began to stray
Towards the calm ocean
And a quiet bay

A rusty yacht sailed by
But no one could be heard
Sophie called towards the boat
But there was not a word.

Gingerly she approached the boat
Worried to look inside
She raised her foot
In her next breath the boat had vanished with the tide.

Abigail Boyle (9)
Elizabeth College Junior School - Beechwood, St. Peter Port

Travelling On Train Dreamland

In my dream I see a fright,
A monster and a vampire in a fight.

In the East,
I see a beast.

A dog in flight
What's in my sight?

I see a brute,
An ugly shoot.

In the devastated waterfall,
I see some ugly cannon balls.

Nice smile,
Crocodile.

I see a cat in a chair,
What are you doing there?

In my wake,
I see a lake.

In the night
I see a light.

I see a glimmer,
and a shimmer.

Soon I wake up tight,
In the middle of the night.

Charlie Forshaw

Elizabeth College Junior School - Beechwood, St. Peter Port

The Dark, Gloomy Room

I stepped into the dark, gloomy room,
And suddenly there was a flash and a boom!
I turned around and there was one way out,
Unfortunately, it was just a tiny little spout!

Through this spout I saw miniscule, green glows,
A few seconds later, there was a tickle on my toes.
I felt into my pockets and found a flashlight,
I switched it on and to my greatest fright...

There were thousands of spiders with glowing eyes,
When I looked at them they turned into some kind of disguise.

Felix Thomas Jack Addenbrooke (9)
Elizabeth College Junior School - Beechwood, St. Peter Port

The Big Crack

There I was on my couch.
I saw my dad and he gave me a fright.
I zoomed up to bed, did my teeth in a second
So when my dad came up I'm like, 'I'm up!'
Then I whacked my head on my wooden bed
And well, I sort of fainted, so off to Dreamland again!
But when I was there I was in a board game.
I was furry,
I... I... I... I... was a Yeti!
Then I saw an elf
Crush him? No!
We ran away on one little adventure
Then I woke up.
I was in hospital
With a cracked head.

Seve Jack Falla (9)
Elizabeth College Junior School - Beechwood, St. Peter Port

A Dream

A dream can be of many kinds,
Leprechauns flying on rainbows
Or becoming a pro footballer.

Maybe flying on dragons,
Or riding unicorns
All seems fun.

But there's a dark side to these wonders,
It all starts well,
Then horrors leap out,
Your heart speeds up
All the fun is gone!

We wonder what these dreams are,
No one seems to know.

But there's a question to ask
To dream or not to dream.
Would you risk it?

Casper Le Ray
Elizabeth College Junior School - Beechwood, St. Peter Port

Nightmares

I went to sleep at seven o' clock one night.
I went to a land of bright white light.

I saw the colour of blood red.
There were ghosts that flooded into my head.

There was a horrible purple river.
I saw some of it strangely glimmer.

I then caught some chickenpox.
The river then turned into a box.

Then a vampire bit my neck
I said, 'Oh what the heck!'

There I lay in my bed
I saw black... was I dead?...

Ralph Humphries (8)
Elizabeth College Junior School - Beechwood, St. Peter Port

The Clown

I found myself in a dark, gloomy building
There were distant screams that were bouncing and
dancing.

What was that? Oh it was just a rat
I was really scared and that's a great fact.

Then I saw it, his pale white face
In his hand was a bloody red mace.

I ran as fast as I possibly could
I thought I would die, I probably would.

Then... I woke up in bed with a big fright
I looked out the window and the sun shone so bright.

George Louis Le Roux (11)
Elizabeth College Junior School - Beechwood, St. Peter Port

Roundabout

The sun shot out, blinding my house,
It was so bright that I can't see my pet mouse.

I went outside and shot the sun,
It was so annoying that it had to be done.

After I turned around, I saw a cute bunny,
It was all alone, so I took it in case anyone would break
its bone.

At the roundabout, it was so dark,
But then I spotted a little spark.

I put my rubbish in the bin,
And I saw this man scratching his chin.

Giulia Rihoy (9)
Elizabeth College Junior School - Beechwood, St. Peter Port

Creepy Monsters

There I lay on top of my bed
Strange creatures dropped into my mind.

The greedy old things
Were so greedy they ripped open a sheep!

There were too many ugly things
A blackbird was near me.

One got closer and closer and closer
and by golly, it was a dragon.

It swooped me up upon its back
And took me to the land of my room.

But I will miss him.
Perhaps I will meet another one?

Rory Clarke (9)
Elizabeth College Junior School - Beechwood, St. Peter Port

Mr Unicorn

In a faraway land
There is a magical unicorn
That lives in a huge land
Of yummy food as yummy as gummy bears
And the skies are full of pies
The trees are made of cheese
He lives in a volcano
And at a press of a button it will erupt funny Fanta
This awesome unicorn flies at night
Trying not to give kids a fright
As the sun goes running up Mr Unicorn flies back to his amazing home
In the faraway world of Unicorn Land.

Will Godfrey (9)
Elizabeth College Junior School - Beechwood, St. Peter Port

I'm A Wizard!

I dreamt I was a wizard,
Bright stars dancing from my stick,
For I was in a huge blizzard,
I got sand off my arm with a flick.

Soon the blizzard was no more,
I was cold, frozen and shivering,
I felt like visiting Dumbledore,
I felt stunned but at least blizzards are water saving.

I soon woke up in bed,
I was feeling dead.
I ran to my mum shouting
'I'm a wizard!'

William Fysh (10)
Elizabeth College Junior School - Beechwood, St. Peter Port

The Best Dream

I was lying in my bed
When some strange dreams came into my head.

I was in a dream with my brother
Then I saw a unicorn with another.

I saw a thing, it looked like a frog
And then a cat that barked like a dog.

Suddenly, a rainbow appeared
Then my dad came in with a bright blue beard.

Then I woke up from my dream
I was late for school, and my mum was mean.

Declan Andrew Crowther-Martel (9)
Elizabeth College Junior School - Beechwood, St. Peter Port

I Hate Clowns!

I have always hated clowns, they make me scared
inside.
I want them out of my system, I want them out of my
mind.
I don't feel good around them, I'd really rather not
See them at all, never mind a lot.

Watching them really scares me, it creeps me out.
I always dream about clowns creeping in my house
I hear them going up the stairs, opening the door
Then I woke up from dreaming on the floor!

Jack Becker (10)
Elizabeth College Junior School - Beechwood, St. Peter Port

The Jar Of Dreams

There was once a jar of extraordinary dreams
Which may sound as weird as it seems.

There were dreams that were sneezy, alive from the
dead.
Dreams that would make you uneasy in your bed.

Some of these dreams would make you smile.
Some would make you scared for a while

But even though these dreams may be bad
Some of which would make you feel glad!

Alexa Annan (9)
Elizabeth College Junior School - Beechwood, St. Peter Port

The Llama Party

We had a party,
The llama seemed arty
The candyfloss giggled,
When I jiggled.

The crocodile rapped away,
We played all day,
Until the sun came up,
We played with the pup.

The cake was there,
Standing with a pear,
It tasted like cheese,
With peas,
Our party had a crazy theme,
And that was the end of our fantastic dream!

Grace Clark (9)
Elizabeth College Junior School - Beechwood, St. Peter Port

The Magic Box

There I was, as bored as a snail
Snoring as loud as a middle-aged male.
Suddenly, I saw a monster that gave a scream!
I was having a very bad dream.
My feet were covered in my old grey socks.
My toes were pointing out like ancient rocks
Then I saw a big box.
I climbed on inside and found myself at home eating
breakfast.
Then I told my mum about that magic box.

Jack Gilbey (8)
Elizabeth College Junior School - Beechwood, St. Peter Port

The Little Elf

In a faraway land,
There lived a little elf,
Who lived in a cottage,
All by himself.

So then he went out to find a friend
Because he felt it was the end,
After he went back to relax,
But his house needed a mend.

Soon after a deer came little,
Elf didn't look the same
He had a mug and he had a,
Toy called Rain.

Jack Meerveld (10)
Elizabeth College Junior School - Beechwood, St. Peter Port

Superman

S uperman where are you? I
U nderstand that you come every night
P lease, please come tonight!
E very night I think about you
R un, come, I hope you can hear me
M aybe you're visiting someone else for a change
A nd then you'll come to me again
N ow Superman, please come super quick, now, now, now!

Rupert Wilson (9)

Elizabeth College Junior School - Beechwood, St. Peter Port

Volcano

V iolent as a lion hunting its prey

O utstanding as a man who has won ten gold medals

L oud as a howler monkey sitting in a tree

C an explode like the world's most powerful bomb

A wesome as the world's best fidget spinner

N ever even as quiet as a mouse

O ut of this world, as a rocket ship in outer space.

Sam Romer (10)
Elizabeth College Junior School - Beechwood, St. Peter Port

Spinosaurus

Your spine is spiky like the tip of an arrow
Your teeth are as sharp as razor blades.
You are the most skilled hunter
You are the best and you win the fight
You are my favourite
Give the rest a fright, show them how to do it.
Show them what's right
The only one that can defeat you.
Is a meteor, it wipes you out.
That must be sore!

Yannick Carpentier
Elizabeth College Junior School - Beechwood, St. Peter Port

The Worst Nightmare!

I fell asleep one night
Then I had a big fright.

I saw a giant snake.
I really wanted to wake.

I felt a tickle on my toe
Then a skeleton pulled back his bow.

The arrow flew through the air.
And trimmed off the top of my hair.

Then I was on a dark track.
Then it was all pitch-black.

Hugo Allen (8)
Elizabeth College Junior School - Beechwood, St. Peter Port

My Dream

I had a dream
which before, I'd never seen
And I was very keen
to figure out
what it was all about.
So I wandered and wobbled
and shouted, then doubted
and came across a castle
made out of rainbows
and a stable
made out of cables
and a knight
who had a flight
in the night
with a kite.

Jacky Marquis (9)
Elizabeth College Junior School - Beechwood, St. Peter Port

Jack T

J ack T one day decided he would play

A nd went to the toy box to find his Santa sleigh

C ross was he, he couldn't find it and he lay on a box from Santa Fe,

K icked the box in a tantrum, it was his lucky month of May

T ight were his trousers, it was just his unlucky day.

Oliver Bloor (9)

Elizabeth College Junior School - Beechwood, St. Peter Port

Horrible Dreams

That night as I lay fast asleep in my bed
Horrible thoughts flooded into my head
Scary clowns, poisonous snakes,
Gathered at the bottom of blood-red lakes.

I then found myself in mysterious lands
Purple skies and scary hands
Evil creatures coming into my room
Coming in to seal my doom.

Sam Savory (9)
Elizabeth College Junior School - Beechwood, St. Peter Port

Pegasus

I see it gliding gracefully
through the romantic sky,
it lands with as much effort
as we put into walking,
I follow it into the lush green
mangrove of palm trees.

Then he swoops effortlessly
to a cold, damp cove.
Suddenly, I wake up in my version of
a cave... my bed.

Will Horsbrugh-Porter (11)
Elizabeth College Junior School - Beechwood, St. Peter Port

The Elf

One day in a faraway land
There was an elf all by himself
His pet was a dragon
Who pulled a wagon
He also had a pet pug
Who drank from a mug
There was a mare
Who ate a pear in his underwear
The blue skies
Were full of pies
The elves' eyes
Were full of lies.

Toby James McIntosh (9)
Elizabeth College Junior School - Beechwood, St. Peter Port

The Deadly Dreams

D aring devils crawling down my back
R earing horses ready to ride in the black
E yes from a wolf staring at me from behind the rock
A ll the wolves just give them a knock
M alls sell hay for the horses of Wonderberg
S ome dreams can go a long, long way.

Charlie Reuben Tourtel (9)
Elizabeth College Junior School - Beechwood, St. Peter Port

The Magical Dream

There I lay fast asleep in my bed
I flickered on my lights to see what was ahead
I noticed a strange little man in the corner.
He looked like he'd stepped out of a sauna.
His eyes were bright,
Suddenly, I was with my big toys back in my bed.
Then all I saw was black, was I dead?

Joe James (9)
Elizabeth College Junior School - Beechwood, St. Peter Port

In My Dreams

M agical Monsters
O ver the world
N ever stopping to find you
S oon they will find you
T oo soon they will find you so
E very night you stick tight to your bed sheets
R eally scary monsters
S een all through the night.

Hugo Le Clerc
Elizabeth College Junior School - Beechwood, St. Peter Port

My Dream

I had a dream
Which had never been seen
And there was a duck which was very keen
Eating a big bean
Also it was on a lead
And had a big deed
To roll on a big red bead
And then I woke up in a stampede.

Yannick Gaudion (9)
Elizabeth College Junior School - Beechwood, St. Peter Port

Tanker

T here was a dwarf on the porch
A nd a bell in a cell
N ine lives, nine pies
K ind times
E nd is near
R un till you dream.

Henry George Swanson (11)
Elizabeth College Junior School - Beechwood, St. Peter Port

Dream Poetry

I go to sleep on a cold winter's night
Every night I take a flight
To a magical land,
Where I meet a magical man.

George Peter Harris (10)
Elizabeth College Junior School - Beechwood, St. Peter Port

How I Saved The School

As I met the flying spider, I realised I was dreaming
It was spying over the quaky sea
Looking for the dusty school, it searched until bed
When I got it out my head.

Everything went straight ahead
The school was in a terrible state
Then the spider stumbled and made a house fall
Making it closer, it got as tall as the school.

Oliver threw a knife
because it tried to strike
Cam bazooka'd its legs
As the spider begged for mercy.

We blew him up
As we flew
Seeing the world shaded
The spider's eyes faded.

Then I woke up in my bed
As safe as I said
Waiting for a new day
In my favourite place to stay.

Alexander Herbert (10)
Parkland Junior School, Eastbourne

Ghost

I see a ghost next to that host over there.
Don't care or it might scare.
He went over there, well do I get a bear to attack?
No, I get a sack, don't worry I'll take your back.
I know a ghost hunter to lead us to a haunted house.
Look there is a mouse.
Let's go in, watch out, there is a bin full of ghosts, the most I've seen.
This place is so clean.
Don't press that beepy button because you will summon a ghost.
Why do I care? I'm not shy!
Because you might die.
Don't be dumb, some people don't believe us.
Look, there's the bus, quick go catch it before we get stuck here.
I'll pay today, so say OK.

Izzie Gray (9)
Parkland Junior School, Eastbourne

The Big Fat Bat

Once I had a dream of a big fat bat,
He flew around my room and landed on a mat,
I screamed and screamed and screamed until he flew
away,
And then I said, 'Wow! That was a strange day!'
I woke up in a shock and stayed up for an hour.
Until I went back to bed and dreamt of a flower.
The next dream I had was of a rat,
He went in circles around a cat.
The cat then ran away because it was scared.
And the rat really, really cared.
The cat was in a box, trembling in fright.
While the rat came up to it with a kite.
The rat said, 'Come on, let's play?'
So the cat came out and said, 'Hip hip hooray!'

Macie Smith (11)
Parkland Junior School, Eastbourne

Famous Dancers

F abulous dresses that dance in the night
A mazing dancers that sing in the light
M y favourite dancer is probably me!
O h I am the best dancer that there can be
U sually there is someone trying to be like me
S o I must go to a dance-off and I will win!

D elightful dresses, I could not pick which one to wear
A nd I have one minute to pick
N o, I don't have much time with this one
C urly hair, that's what I need
E very time I do my hair I forget to feed
R uby my dog, the cutest puppy in the world
S o now it is time for my dance-off.

Isabella Parmley (8)
Parkland Junior School, Eastbourne

Nightmare

Last night I fell in a deep,
Into a slumber of sleep,
It was a shame I wasn't counting sheep.

I knew I wasn't alone,
although I knew my friend was me,
But I swear there was something else I could see,
Then I heard a piercing scream,
it was my friend Jamie-Leigh.

I turned around
to see three clowns
the middle one was bigger
and was about to pull a gun trigger
the other two had knives
Was this going to be the end of our lives?

Last night I fell in deep
Into a slumber of sleep
It was a shame it wasn't a dream.

Millie Barker (11)
Parkland Junior School, Eastbourne

Monster

M etal dragon transforming into monsters blowing up trucks and houses straight into flames.

O minous creature coming out of the darkness like a great white shark. Its enormous metal teeth crushing through rock like it's not there.

N uclear rockets flying out of the army tanks trying to hit the monster, but the monster just avoiding the nuclear rockets and blowing up the army tank.

S corching flames everywhere, burning everything it touches.

T errified people run from the horror.

E veryone's screaming and shouting.

R ampage of abomination.

Max Perry (8)
Parkland Junior School, Eastbourne

Slime

Slime is stretchy, pokeable and heavy.
I feel excited to make it fluffy.
My friends and I are dancing around.
We're laughing and getting ready now.
Slime, slime, it's never lost it's fun
Everyone is gathering round.
Let's make it stretchy.
Slime, slime, slime, it's stretchy, poke able
and also fluffy.

Slime, slime it's so much fun,
We're all standing under the sun
Stirring and spraying and waiting for it to be done.
Emma, Holly, Mya, Amber and Lauren,
mixing and mixing to get it all done.

Holly (11) & Emma Furminger
Parkland Junior School, Eastbourne

At Midnight!

A s dark as dungeons, as scary as night, I tiptoe into my room with joy and excite,

T houghts in my head, what's in my bed?

M idnight's manic and dreadful too but nothing compares to what I'm up to

I llusion images flash into fear

D readful dreams will soon appear

N auseous noises all around

I must be inside a dreadful clown

G asping for air

H itting, bashing, boom, someone help me soon

T his could be the end of me if I don't get out of this dream!

Chloe Haizelden (10)
Parkland Junior School, Eastbourne

Cliffhanger

We're in Millie's basement,
Making a lot of slime,
Of course, we're going home soon,
So we're running out of time!

We need more glue,
to make this thing work,
Come on guys,
Let's go search!

We scampered around the whole basement,
looking for glue
when Lily found a sheet and pulled it off...

'Get up!' Mum shouted, 'You're late for school!'
Wait, it was just a dream and Mum had woke me up!
Not cool!

Jamie-Leigh Barnaville-Gibbs (11)
Parkland Junior School, Eastbourne

My School Dream

I woke up and saw a big school
This was old school
I went in there and saw all my friends
I felt cold but happy.

But my friends looked very scared
They all were just looking at a wall
I felt very light
I looked down at the floor
I was flying up in the air
I was nearly in space
I could see the world
I didn't want to wake up.

I was flying all night
I didn't want to stop
I wish my friends were there
So I could have more fun.

Cem Ali Çetin (10)
Parkland Junior School, Eastbourne

Builder

B ouncing around, I saw a builder building a hotel

U nder a rock there was an angry, ominous creature waiting for his prey to rest.

I had to go to save him or he was going to be in a midnight feast

L eaping in, I told the person making the hotel to run

D amping down his bricks, he told me to go away.

E xactly at nine o'clock I said to myself, 'It's been a long day.'

R eally tired, I wrapped myself in my covers and went to sleep.

Josh Young (8)
Parkland Junior School, Eastbourne

Space Race

I get into my rocket made of steel,
My brother is with me, he's super excited,
The engines roar and rattle,
Off we go into space,
We're going to have a race.

Like a tornado the Milky Way spins,
Stars fly past like racers,
We land on a planet as big as the sun,
We're in space having a race,
Back to the rocket,
Past all of the stars and the Milky Way,
Back to Earth, into bed,
I wake up,
We were in space having a race!

Fraser Robert Mechan (10)
Parkland Junior School, Eastbourne

Lionel Messi

His boots looked at him
Like a shining light in the dark.

He ran onto the football pitch
The El Clásico was here.

Ronaldo looked at him
like a hawk.

The match began,
His lovely son was
Cheering, 'Messi, Messi, Messi!'

Ten minutes left, still 0-0
Messi ran with the ball, the ball was a bird,
he smashed the ball from the halfway line
And what a goal!
What a crazy dream!

Leon Wilkinson (9)
Parkland Junior School, Eastbourne

The Amazing Horse

My horse is like a unicorn.
It is blue, indigo, red and yellow
My horse jumps over tall, thick trees,
And it gallops really fast.

I was riding on the Downs.
The horse went on its back legs,
And shot into the sky like a rocket.
I felt terrified, but it was fun at the same time.

Fluffy clouds were above me.
I landed on a cloud in the shape of a horse.
Gravity pulled me back to Earth,
The horse ran off into the sunset.

Alfie William Young (10)
Parkland Junior School, Eastbourne

Forest Fire

Trees, trees, trees, an endless path of trees,
Gravel path leading through the forest trees with leaves
On top of a tree sat a mat
On the mat was a cat with a bat.
The ginger cat fell and died,
Whilst I had fun with my hair that was dyed,
I made it to the cove as a dragon,
Started to breathe fire to another dragon,
The fire started to spread,
Like spreading butter on bread,
I ran down the path,
then I woke up and had a bath.

Rhys Binks (11)
Parkland Junior School, Eastbourne

In The Sky

Once I went to bed
And felt a strong knock on my head
I woke up to feast my eyes
On a world way up in the skies
I went around greeting
And even saw someone sleeping...
Then I saw the queen
And could tell she was not mean
Then I heard my name announced
And everybody began to shout
I never knew what they would have said
But I felt something in my bed
I was having so much fun
But then my dream was done.

Cerys Andrews (9)
Parkland Junior School, Eastbourne

Deadly Tomatoes

Deadly tomatoes everywhere
Each day I think deadly things
All day, until one day, I am all alone in my
Deadly room, then I heard a deadly tomato, squash!
I thought it was just me.
Then I went shopping
And saw the deadly tomato following me.
Its eyes were as blue as the ocean,
As red as blood teeth like shark teeth
I ran shouting, 'Get out, get out!' It tried to eat them,
Stomp, dead!

Alex Andrew Modestou (8)
Parkland Junior School, Eastbourne

All Alone

All alone, in the wood, clowns,
Red-eyed unicorns, spiders, evil wizards
And bats that fly make me cry!

Terrible teachers
And pompous pirates give me a fright!

Dangerous dancers pick me up a fight.
Clownarius clowns puff out clouds at me!

I choke and hurt, then suddenly I feel no hurt...
I'm now very scared no one around,
I'm now truly all alone.

Angel Leigh Masters (10)
Parkland Junior School, Eastbourne

Monster

M etal dragon is out! I don't know where it is, like a survival hunt for a lot of meat

O minous metal dragon and we're terrified to go outside, it is a bad decision

N ike shoes on the monster and hiding its vicious claws

S cary monster in the bushes

T errific adventure, I have got a big army

E normous monster, here you go

R eptile, I don't like this...

Will Smith (7)

Parkland Junior School, Eastbourne

Clowns

E very one is frightened
V ery hard to see
I wonder if there are clowns
L urking near me

C lown's red shoes squeak on the forest floor
L eaves rustling on their feet
O n the trees are mysterious letters
W hat do they mean?
N ervously they turn and scream
S houting from the treetops, they chase.

Bailey Ashdown (10)
Parkland Junior School, Eastbourne

Dragon

A dragon as strong as a body builder
He looks like Lego in Lego World
Fire and acid he can breath
He can morph into anything he wants
Oh, and that dragon's name is Noah!
He morphs into a human and goes to school
He gets put into a noisy Year Six class
A teacher he meets is very tall
The class mates are scared of me,
because when I'm angry I turn into a dragon.

Noah Impey (11)
Parkland Junior School, Eastbourne

James Time

J ames Bang! James Bang!
A red iron helmet communicating to the satellite
M ad like an angry dog
E lastic suit that's indestructible
S uperhero smash! Superhero smash!

T all like a washing-up robot
I 'm the king of the world!
M agnificent like a mouse
E ating like a posh man.

James Snashall (8)
Parkland Junior School, Eastbourne

Deadly Dreams!

D angerous, dark,
E xcitement, gone
A lone or are you?
D eadly creatures
L ike a drum, the thunder bangs!
Y our heart pumping

D ead spider comes to life
R ed glaring eyes
E eek!
A rgh!
M adness in my head,
S top! I've fallen out of bed!

Hebe Warren (10)
Parkland Junior School, Eastbourne

Gamer's Glitch

Rayman's lost arcade machine
This must be a gamer's dream.
I get sucked in
Ninety-nine goblins to save a king?
Lucy must help King Ping.
We hunt, twelve remain,
The gamer glitch.
One boss to defeat.

We've lost all our lives
No hope remains
Let's go to Atlantis
City of the sea!

Kieran Hayward (8)
Parkland Junior School, Eastbourne

My Demon Neighbour

Hello neighbour, I'm in your house.
You'll never find me, I'm like a mouse
I hide in cupboards and in your fridge
'Are you creepy, are you not?'
'That is for you to find out.'
'I need your secrets, you sad devil.'
'You'll never find me, I'm like a mouse rebel.'

Django Swanmens
Parkland Junior School, Eastbourne

The Best Goal Ever

One day I had a dream
With football and fairies and fame
I prayed and prayed
Oh please, oh please
Just let me win this game
A fairy came down and dabbed me with
Her wand of wish and dream
You can score a goal
So go for it kid now's your chance
You're winning the game victory.

Amelia Bernard (9)
Parkland Junior School, Eastbourne

My Worst Nightmare

Running, running, running
Rushing through the forest
My worst nightmare,
Thoughts in my head
I turn around
I see him, the clown
Behind him is a demon
Running, running, running
Why did I get in this bed?
Help, help, help.
The clown is whiter than white
But I wake in my bed.

Ted Brickley (9)
Parkland Junior School, Eastbourne

Bruno Gets Powers

Last night I had an amazing dream
Running on a pitch
Feeling excited
Kicking a soft ball
Scoring goals.

In my dream
I meet Saltor Bruno

In my dream
Bruno got a power
To be giant
Bang! Crash!
Running through the pitch.

Rory Arbenz (9)
Parkland Junior School, Eastbourne

Dog And A Hog

The dog said to the hog,
'What a very nice log.'
The rat said to the cat,
'What a very nice hat.'
Then the fish said to the dish,
'I want to make a wish.'
Then the clock said to the rock,
'Tick-tock!'

What a crazy dream.

Grace Bredemeier-Maher (8)
Parkland Junior School, Eastbourne

Future Dream

Flying cars and hover cycles
A robot friend by my side
Excited, anxious and scared
We are in the future
No wonder where
Running from robo cops
As fast as a cheetah
With a rocket launcher and disrupter
Boom! The cops are gone
We succeeded in our mission!

Thomas Elliott (9)
Parkland Junior School, Eastbourne

Demon's Leg

Demon's leg
staring at me,

Demon's leg
belongs to a dragon,

Demon's leg
is red.

Demon's leg
has an eye,

Demon's leg,
so small and dead

Demon's leg
what are you?

Zak Adams (9)
Parkland Junior School, Eastbourne

Famous

F lying so high was a star singing lovely
A mazingly, a magic music box flew into my hands
M agic is in dreams and fun, so be a star
O ne day I will be a singing star
U nless I fail my singing test
S ummer is the best month to sing and dance.

Kacie-Leigh Lambert (8)
Parkland Junior School, Eastbourne

The Monster Teacher

Last night I had a dream and it all started at school.
We had a new teacher who looked like a monster.
Could this day get any worse?

It was the end of the day
she spoke to me, I walked away.
Hooray, that's the end of the day.
No more of that teacher.

Dylan White (9)
Parkland Junior School, Eastbourne

Lovely

L uscious flowing, blowing in the wind
O nly a group of two can have true happiness
V iolet had a whole box of sticky chewing gum
E aster eggs are as yummy as smoothies
L ovely is as nice as a princess
Y ummy ice cream is super delicious.

Phoenix Ana Parker
Parkland Junior School, Eastbourne

The Nightmare

Eerie shadows lurk behind twisted trees,
Creepy figures all around,
Suddenly, I hear a noise,
I turn around and what do I see?

A mythical creature,
With piercing eyes,
A wart upon her nose,
Tongue as black as coal.

A nightmare?

Ella Perry (10)
Parkland Junior School, Eastbourne

Candyland

It's full of sweets in Dreamland
The clouds are full of fluff
The paths are made of chocolate
The taste is not enough
It's wonderful in Dreamland
There's a lot of ice cream
I don't want to leave this place
Oh no, it's all a dream.

Zach Thomas (10)
Parkland Junior School, Eastbourne

Rescue Brigade

R ush, there's an emergency
E mergency services dash to the disaster
S creaming fire engines lights flash like lightning
C an they make it on time?
U mmm, beeped the ambulance
E veryone stop and stare as the vehicles go past.

Finley Goldsmith (8)
Parkland Junior School, Eastbourne

Dragons

D ark deadly flames came falling like a skydiver
R oars like a dinosaur dying
A dventurous hunter
G rabs and gobbles his gory prey
O rangey red fiery flames whooshed from his mouth
N asty as an alligator
S caly body.

Aiden Barnaville-Gibbs (7)

Parkland Junior School, Eastbourne

Flying

F ar in the sky, blue like the sea
L istening to the radio, bobbing my head
Y awning flies, living free
I nternational flights, flying high
N ever looking down from their monitor
G liding through the fluffy clouds, like a hawk.

Archie George Taylor (8)
Parkland Junior School, Eastbourne

Untitled

Now, now you naughty cow
Your behaviour has been very foul
Before my eyes I could see,
A big ugly ogre called Lee.
He was located in a pot
With a unicorn, formally the whole lot.
The ogre was ginger from head to toe
But one thing was he was very slow.

Tom Nerhati (10)
Parkland Junior School, Eastbourne

Jeloids

J elly! Wobbling on his head
E gg sweats on his back
L egs made of shortbread
O range-tasting rings on his feet
I ngredients in his hands
D ividing, sharing his ingredients
S crumdiddlyumptious shortbread body.

Harry Jupp (8)
Parkland Junior School, Eastbourne

Spiders

S pooky spider big as a giraffe
P uts me in its mouth
I find myself inside its gut
D oes death await me now?
E verywhere are creepy flies
R umble, gurgle, slosh...
S pider's sick - I'm safe!

Oscar Lindfield (10)
Parkland Junior School, Eastbourne

The Getaway Pirates

P lease, please leave me alone.
I 'm not safe here on my own
R ob our ship without a care
A t sea or anywhere
T each you a lesson you must learn
E asy to burn you
S o never come back and never return!

Nomi Alicia Oakley (9)
Parkland Junior School, Eastbourne

Fairies

F luttering beautiful fairies
A mazing, joyful, colourful wings like a butterfly
I maginary friends
R escuing magical creatures
I nhabitant mushrooms in the forest
E xcited to play
S oft, glittery wings.

Grace Kelly (8)
Parkland Junior School, Eastbourne

Pretty Pirate

P retty pirate loved sailing in the shimmering sea
I like you pretty pirate
R eally she doesn't know anything
A nd she doesn't even know what
T oday is. I am surprised!
E veryone else is surprised too!

Jasmine Jakeman (8)
Parkland Junior School, Eastbourne

On A Submarine

I once had a dream,
Where I rode a submarine
Down there I found some chickens,
From a book written by Charles Dickens.
I saw an underwater crow,
And a fish wearing a bright pink bow.
I was on a submarine,
When I had this crazy dream.

Cara Lewis (8)
Parkland Junior School, Eastbourne

Spiders

S campering up the drainpipe
P owerfully pulls himself up the pipe
I nsects turn away as quick as a cheetah
D angles near my head like rain
E ating bugs
R unning up a tree
S ilently watching.

Rhyley Willott (8)
Parkland Junior School, Eastbourne

Spiders

S ticky spiders every day
P oisonous, in your way
I ts web felt like ice in my hair.
D anger in the way
E very day, they die
R un fast as you can
S pitting poisonous spit.

Donte Adams (7)
Parkland Junior School, Eastbourne

Clowns

C reeping across the hall
L ike a cat in the middle of the night
O ver the wooden floorboard creak, creak, creak
W hen I hear a creak I get under my covers
N owhere to hide and nowhere to run.

Ime Emerald Janine Cox (8)
Parkland Junior School, Eastbourne

Clowns

Haunted house in the wood,
Loud screams from within
Creepy faces stare at me
Like fog floating around
Too scared to go inside
Turn and run away
Clowns jump from the swaying trees,
Crash! I fall and die!

Max Theo Nightingale (10)
Parkland Junior School, Eastbourne

Dragons

D eadly fire from his mouth
R umbles in his tummy
A rmour made of scales
G nashes his teeth
O verpowering roars can be heard
N oise like thunder
S hadows scare everyone.

Max Ryan Oliver Gilbert (8)
Parkland Junior School, Eastbourne

Rich As Can Be

Rich as can be,
I board a private jet
My yacht is moored in the harbour
And money in the bank!
Lavish cars on my drive
Tell of wealth-like things...
You know I'm only dreaming about exotic things!

Liam Delacy (10)
Parkland Junior School, Eastbourne

Dear Unicorn

Above me you fly,
Like a rainbow in the sky,
Your eyes are so bright,
Like stars in the night.
You live in Dream Land,
Where candyfloss is sand,
Your magic is true,
I wish I could be with you.

Jamie Keira Da Silva (10)
Parkland Junior School, Eastbourne

The Unwanted Unicorn

In my dream
When I was five
A vicious unicorn
Who wasn't wanted for anything,
Came to my house,
It asked me if I wanted a ride.
I said, 'Yes of course.'
He took me to Cake Land.

Ava Belle Woodrow (8)
Parkland Junior School, Eastbourne

Teacher

T earing like mad
E verywhere a mess
A ngry and shouting
C hildren sobbing and weeping
H avoc and mayhem
E rupting like an earthquake
R un everywhere.

Stanley Forder (8)
Parkland Junior School, Eastbourne

Teacher

T he teacher was horrible
E very day she was grumpy
A s mean as a beast
C alling children
H aving to run
E xtreme PE
R unning home.

Josh Fox (7)
Parkland Junior School, Eastbourne

Goo Factory

I live in a goo factory
Goo monsters are cross with me,
I came here through the sewers
They smelt like rotten eggs
How can I get out of here
And back home to my bed?

Curtis John Bint (10)
Parkland Junior School, Eastbourne

Killer Clown

Killer clown runs through the night
Smashing doors and breaking lights
With its powerful laugh
And evil stare,
But lucky for us
Killer clowns are rare!

Ben Wilkinson (10)
Parkland Junior School, Eastbourne

Dreams

D aring quests
R unning from Bandits
E vil demons
A ttacked by bears
M eeting ancient leaders
S uddenly, I wake up.

Ella Waters (10)
Parkland Junior School, Eastbourne

Puppy

P ouncing everywhere
U nder and over leaves
P laying with a ball
P ulling on a rope
Y awning now and feeling sleepy.

Lucas Leonard Brown (8)
Parkland Junior School, Eastbourne

The Alien Invasion

Outside my house glistens, a bright light
I put my shoes on, laces tied up tight
My friend joins me, to discover this new thing
We saw an alien with a diamond ring.

The alien was like a gorilla, very tough
Also like a lion, extremely rough
'Quick,' yelled my friend, 'grab that golden ring'
That's probably why it's as powerful as the king.

I had it in my hand
And threw it on the land
It broke and went *bang!*
The alien had gone, we celebrated, we sang.

We didn't tell anyone about this invasion
It was in a secret location
We went home.
And winked at each other as we landed in Rome.

Jessica Steele (9)
Portesham CE Primary School, Portesham

The Dragon Astronauts And The Castle

On a sky island floating high
A tree looks really sly
I gaze down at a dragon in a castle
Suddenly, *smack!* I get hit by a flying parcel.

I open it and find a five pence piece
On the front is my grandma's fleece
I wondered where it came from but suddenly, *whoosh!*
Something gave me a push.

I strongly float down
Then I see eight astronauts, one with a crown
They said, 'Hi.'
I said, 'Bye!'
Then seconds later, I land at the castle.
Tinimo the guard dragon woke up and yelled, 'Rascal!'
Suddenly, the king astronaut came to rescue me
When we got home we were just in time for tea!

Riffe Bradley (9)
Portesham CE Primary School, Portesham

The Run From Annabelle

Happy, I skipped to the ticket line
Suddenly, Annabelle the ghost jumped out, she looked about nine
No one else saw her, I was shocked, I raced away
I wasn't going to stop till I saw the bay.

Nobody went there so I turned a corner fast
I was then trapped, I remembered she was in the past
Trying all the doors, they were all locked
Annabelle was closing in on me, I was blocked.

She was coming faster, I tried one more door
It opened, I ran in, there were bones on the floor
Suddenly, a door appeared, I jumped in quickly
It wasn't a room, it was an imaginary land where no cake was sickly.

Evie Bull (9)
Portesham CE Primary School, Portesham

The Giant's Stomach

Gazing down the never-ending tube,
Staring, thinking about the colourful cube
Fairies dancing on the caramel trees
Busy, little bumblebees.

Excited about discovering
Curious about uncovering
Smiling, dancing flowers,
And chocolate chip showers.

An elf making friends with me
We love to drink weird-flavoured tea
This land is as wonderful as ice cream
They even have an amazing football team.

Candyfloss clouds dance in the huge sun
Creatures always are having fun
The pond is full of rainbowfish
Make a wonderful, dream-filled wish.

Florence Farnham (8)
Portesham CE Primary School, Portesham

Pegasuses

Pegasuses flying way up high
Whooshing around the galaxy sky.
Rainbow magic in their horns
They are flying unicorns.

Pegasuses show a lovely light
Keeping everyone safe from fright.
Sparkles flying everywhere
Blasting off in the air.

If you see a shooting star
It means they are not far.
When the sun comes up they hide
And if you're lucky you may catch a ride.

They are great.
Don't expect them to hesitate.
It's magical when they're seen
Pegasuses are very keen.

Charlotte Burgess (9)
Portesham CE Primary School, Portesham

A Dream Away

As I gaze up at the morning sky
I see a dragon ready to fly
The gooey goodness in the chocolate lake
My mum and dad are baking a cake.

When I wander across the land
I can see a patch of sand
The dragon is as angry as a bull
Also, its tummy is extremely full.

The unicorn flies above the stars
Then goes to Mars
Then gives me a ride on its back
All my friends are carrying a heavy sack.

The two lands collide
And we were all on one side.
We all jump in the candyfloss
There is no loss!

Sulis Baird (9)
Portesham CE Primary School, Portesham

A Day In A Dream

A day in a dream, what a wonderful glow,
Anyway, we never get to play in the snow
Let's travel so far,
But not by car.

When I got there, what did I see,
A famous footballer staring at me
Where was this place?
It looked ace.

A day in a dream, how good to know,
Is the footballer going to go?
'I think not,' he said,
As he turned his head.

As the footballer came towards me,
I was filled with glee
As I went home,
He asked, 'Are you alone?'

Gracie Summers (9)
Portesham CE Primary School, Portesham

The Land Of Sweets And Fairies!

The night sky is filled with shining stars
Many dreams in tiny jars
I go to bed and close my eyes
Wake up to a magic surprise.

Tiny people climbing up candy canes
Baby unicorns and their pretty pink manes
Flowers blooming, across the land
Lovely to watch, how very grand.

The houses are made of chocolate and sweets
As you go in the houses they are tidy and neat
Magical power came through my hands
Screaming and shouting in this world is banned.

Trinity McCann (9)
Portesham CE Primary School, Portesham

A Helping Hand

When I entered this wonderful land,
Two mythical creatures gave me a helping hand
I am a baby monkey and I am playing in the sand
With two mythical creatures that gave me a helping
hand.

Space unicorn has a huge horn,
And it was the same size when he was born
Chimpanzee riding on a Segway,
Thinks it's so big that he has to look away.

They took me to places
Like car races,
And that's why a helping hand,
Is always grand.

Sullie Yelland (9)
Portesham CE Primary School, Portesham

Where Are You?

Mrs Fairy, where are you?
Have you gone to the zoo?
Are you coming back
Do you have a snack?

Where have you gone?
I can't mow the lawn!
So please will you come
Have you hurt your thumb?

Are you still my friend
To the end?
Do you have any money
To buy some honey?

Tell me where are you?
Have you gone to the loo?
You are late
But you're still my mate!

Daisy McCarthy (8)
Portesham CE Primary School, Portesham

Bulgaria's Beach

B ulgaria's beach is like chippings of a golden trophy
U nless villains attack Bulgaria's world
L akes are rainbow-coloured and cars hover
G reat is my friend, he protected me and died, but he came back
A hole in the ground, I wonder what it is?
R ight now I will go home for a nap
I 've just woken up, I walk out the door but its gone
Ab urglar has been I think.

Jake Stone (9)
Portesham CE Primary School, Portesham

Football Pitch

I'm sat alone
Having a moan
We lost our game
Because we were being lame.

We lost against fame
In the pouring rain
That is what happened last May
That's all I want to say.

I'm now sitting in the sun
Having lots of fun
I'm no longer glum
I can't believe I was so dumb!

Evie Prior (8)
Portesham CE Primary School, Portesham

Candy Land

I always lean
Into my dream
When I came in like this
It always has a twist.

It is such a mist
After unicorns have kissed
They hurt my wrist
In the mist.

When I wake up
I'm in a cup
There is a cat
On the mat.

Dreams are fun for everyone!

Lexie Garland (7)
Portesham CE Primary School, Portesham

I Am An Athlete

All the athletes in the world
Taking their dream one step further,
Handing good luck to their teammates.
'Let me win,' I said, in my dream.
Eat a good meal before I start.
Let the swimming race begin.
Towards the finish line, I am going, yes!
I won first place.

Megan Burgess (9)
Portesham CE Primary School, Portesham

Candy Land

Candy Land is scrummy
All the cakes are yummy
The clowns are always funny
The sun is always sunny.

There is always light
But not at night
You might get a fright
Don't worry, the unicorns don't bite
Have a nice night
Snuggle up tight.

Imogen Lilly Baber (9)
Portesham CE Primary School, Portesham

Space

Gazing through the shimmering stars
I can see to blood-red Mars
Astronauts went to the rubber white moon
To see the stars explode. *Boom!*

Space is noiseless and dark,
Not loud and sunny like a park.

Ben Spencer-Veale (7)
Portesham CE Primary School, Portesham

Forests Are Good Or Some Are Bad

F orests are good
O r some are bad
R arely right from wrong
E ast is like a frostbite
S itting down while the trees are making a sound
T ired and relaxed, I sit on the cold ground.

Frank McCarthy (8)
Portesham CE Primary School, Portesham

Royalty

King? Queen? What can you say?
Royalty is soon coming my way.
I will be king and rule the whole country
then no one will ever come above me.

I met my dad and he said, 'Hey.'
I said, 'Dad, will I ever be king one day?'
He said, 'Son, being king isn't everything,
it's the happiness and love you get from parents.'

But I didn't listen and I went on,
was there anything that could be done?
I went to my uncle, (the actual king).
I asked him, 'How did you get such a great living?'
He said, 'It's your father and mother,
they are the reasons why you'll become king!'

My brain exploded and my heart pounded,
I was going to be king... So excited.
Until I heard something above my head,
it was vibrating, shaking, all above my head.
I opened my eyes and let out a scream,
until I realised it was all just a dream.

Khush P Patel (11)
Reddiford School, Pinner

My Best Dream

Last night I had a funny dream.
It's really nothing like it seemed
a planet out of question
I think it was my best one.

Where the spiders only had five legs
where giraffes had one more neck,
animals ruled their world alone
giving dinosaurs space to roam.
Fairies used to eat dried leaves
and lions fed on dying trees.
Dragons breathing out hot fire,
the hippo was a big, fat liar.

The people lived in Humanland,
which was covered with grainy, purple sand
now called Earth, a funny name
from professional athletes to people with fame.
The houses floated in the air,
boys had really, really long hair.
Kings and queens taunted each other
each world was nothing like another.

Fairytale Land is next on the list.
Snow White and the prince finally kissed.
The seven dwarfs, ever so small,
drank a potion, made them very, very tall.
Cinderella dancing up till midnight,
every day, until the clock strikes.
Sleeping Beauty finally woke up
Beauty with the Beast with the talking cup.

The other side of this planet, not so bright.
There were no smiles, no love, no light.
Rumpelstiltskin's name was never guessed
innocent people were accused of theft.

Rapunzel never escaped her tower
all the petals fell from the Beast's flower.
The wolf ate Red Riding Hood
the villains were never defeated, no one would.

Another place, very dark.
A dog with its ferocious bark,
blinking eyes everywhere
giving you a frightful scare.

Large green monsters with one big eye,
'Argh!' a scared, long sigh.
A really big brown bear,
is this only a nightmare?

And then...
I woke up from a dream so bad
but am I relieved or am I sad?
A horrible dream, yes quite such
but oh, I miss that dream so much.

Ria Shah (11)
Reddiford School, Pinner

Deadly Beasts

I was rocking and rocking my head,
Side to side and my whole body was sucked into my
brain,
I woke up in a tropical land, which was really insane.
There were dinosaurs with water legs,
Like scoops of rain and it stomped on me,
I would be in pain.

There was a tiger mixed with a lion,
The skin was splashes of yellow, black and orange
mixed together,
It was like two different animals married.
I think they will be there forever.

Whoosh! A ferocious dragon swooped in the air,
Breathing fire in the hot breeze,
it was gigantic, like God and a giant,
it looked like the deadliest creature which I could see,
its fire poured down from the sky, ready to set ablaze a
creature.

Its beady eyes looked like a blood mouse,
the scales were moist and were dark red.
It breathed more fire which was fired straight at me...
'Argh!' I woke up in my nice, cosy bed.

Caylan Zakharia
Reddiford School, Pinner

Once Upon A Fairy Tale

'Open your eyes!' a voice calls.
I do so and I see some white walls.
'Where am I?' I asked the voice.
My shadow shrugged, having no choice.
I see a bright light coming from nowhere.
'Argh!' I cry in surprise and despair.
Suddenly, I'm tugged in by a strong breeze,
I hear a loud buzz, like a swarm of bees.

I find myself in a gloomy bedroom,
Then the door opens with an intimidating boom!
'What on earth are you doing in my abode?
Trying to steal? Well, I'll turn you into a toad!'
It was the evil queen from the fairy tale!
She wanted to kill me with no fail.

I cried, 'No, please Your Majesty!
I wasn't here to steal, not even a flea!'
'How can I trust you?' she questionably quizzed.
'I came through a portal, I immediately whizzed.
'A portal?' she scoffed. 'What a lie!
Now get ready to say goodbye.'

'Wait, Your Majesty, I propose a deal.
There is nothing I have tried to conceal.
Though I suppose you want Snow White's heart?'
'Yes!' she cried. 'Kill her with a poison dart.'

'But... but, I cannot do such a thing!'
'You will for your life, human being!'
I couldn't believe the queen would threaten me.
Oh no, I thought, *what a tragedy.*
Suddenly my heart started to pound
and then I awoke to a deafening sound.

I saw flashes of the Wicked Witch of the West,
She looked as if she'd been having a guest.
'Oh my gosh!' I gasped. 'Was that me?'
Turns out, the evil Queen was more serious than could
be...

Vedika Rakesh Bhopatrao (11)
Reddiford School, Pinner

The Dream-Mare

Apricots and peaches tinted the sky,
Blossom-tailed peacocks passing by.
Where was I, in a kind of dream?
Are things really so perfect like they seem?

Jellyfish floated through the air,
Their colours dancing here and there,
Rivers rushed like busy streets,
their rapids blue and crystal clean.

Spirits darted through the land,
Like dashes of glitter, one in my hand.
A shimmery breeze and then a well,
Large, grey stones, by age they fell.

My weightless feet stepped over the ocean,
Making ripples to show the surface had awoken.
I left the land, overjoyed, floating on air,
Like a phantom, looking over the dolphins and pears.

Then I arrived in a place brand new.
With there be orchards, mushroom houses too?
'Will I meet someone?' I pondered,
'or is this a world where no one else wanders?'

My wishes were destroyed, my hopes dismissed,
For all I could see was smoky wisps.
Ghosts loom by the trees, their branches bony fingers,
Worry fills my heart, a hanging mist lingers.

I feel piercing eyes gazing into my soul.
When will the bright morning be taking its toll?
Bats loom, a screeching noise,
I'm crumbling apart, collapsing my poise.

Beads of sweat trickled down my face,
My heart is pounding as if in a race.
Blackness closes around me, tiny and scared,
I opened my eyes, at a warm light, I stared.

Eliza Mukhtar (11)
Reddiford School, Pinner

My Job

As the children follow me
to the classroom,
all I hear is chatting.
'What phone do you have?'
'You'll never guess what happened to me.'
'Have you heard of that new game?'

Trying to settle them down,
since maths is approaching.
As I sit down in my big, comfy chair
I reach for the register, the register where is it?
It's close to 9, I'm trying to stay calm, but nobody is
listening.

Bang! I slammed my hand on the desk.
Silence for once.
By 9:15 everything is done.
What's next on the list?
Ah yes, maths.
Addition, what a lovely subject.
'Phil, what is 123+28?'
The numbers just sang out of his mouth,
'151 Miss.'

Finally, English has arrived,
Whoopee!
I'm not teaching.
I head straight for the staffroom,
tea and biscuits are waiting for me.
As I open the door, a bright light flashes in my face,
brighter than the sun.
A big, lovely sofa waiting to be jumped on.
A big, lovely stack of Bourbons and the tea had just
been brewed.

Just then I realised,
No break for me.
A load of marking.
The workload never stops.
This is my life, day after day,
I am a teacher and this is my role.

Aanya Dave
Reddiford School, Pinner

Once Upon An Enchanted Dream

As I prowled into Mystical Wood
as I stood enchanted by the charming beauty
the delicate fairies flew by.
Watching them fly past.

A little gem fell
it was a crystal berry.
Looking up there was an arch covered with crystal
berries,
and unknowing of its unusual powers
I transformed into a fairy.

Fluttering past the delighting aspects
I came to a halt.
There in front of me was a magnificent alicorn
its multicoloured hair waving gently.
Studded on the hair were diamonds
sparkling in the sunlight.

To my surprise, the crystal berry power had faded
away.
I was bursting with joy
I could ride on the alicorn.

As it took flight with me on its back
we soared through the candyfloss clouds
and gummy, blue sky.

As I opened one eye, then the other,
the disappointment exploded.
It was a dream!

Dreaming back to sleep,
I was roaming the mystical woods once more.
Eating and collecting crystal berries
and riding on the alicorn.
Mesmerising, the candyfloss clouds melting in your
mouth,
soaring through my imagination,
leaving the magic behind.

Riyah Solomons
Reddiford School, Pinner

Mystery Land

I open my eyes to find I am sitting on a rock,
I alone upon the big, dirty block
And in front of me is a track,
Suddenly, a cold shiver ran down my back.

I find myself strolling up the track to the top of the
mountain,
Up and up I go, up the steep mountain,
I see a rabbit jump into its burrow,
As the path gets more narrow.

Finally, I reached the top
To find an ice pop.
On the ice pop there was a cave,
Upon the mountain was its grave.

A loud roar shook the ground
And death was where I was to be bound.
Out came the beast,
It shouted, 'You are going to be my feast!'

The beast had an eagle's head
And the front two legs were razor-sharp claws.
The back two legs and body were like a lion,
It had wings of a pegasus and the tail of a snake.

My heart pounded in my breast,
Panic rose in my chest.
The creature knocked me down...
I woke up, was this all a dream now?

Rhea Patel
Reddiford School, Pinner

A Tour By A Unicorn

We floated to an unknown land,
where mystical creatures roamed free.
The land was so fluffy, it was hard to stand,
then a unicorn came, hair dancing in the breeze.

The unicorn took me to the crazy baker
who was preparing a candy meal.
Rolling a pastry under his pin,
as his clumsy assistant slipped on a banana skin.

Then we visited the strong police force,
working on a tricky case,
whilst plotting how to stop the wizards
and tracking their trace.

Then the unicorn took me to the grand palace
made of gingerbread and sweets.
I looked in awe at this beautiful sight
as I chewed on a chocolate treat.

Then I gazed out, back to my bed,
under the blankets nice and cosy.
Then I realised my dream was dead,
but I knew I'd see them again,
because she'll always be my unicorn tour friend!

Zaina Rasiah
Reddiford School, Pinner

The Nightmare Sleepover

N othing could make this day better.

I was with my best friends at a sleepover.

G etting some food for a midnight feast!

H urrying back upstairs.

T hud, bang, drip!

M y friends are gone!

A s afraid as a zebra fleeing from the lion's sharp teeth.

R ed blood dripping on the windows, hand prints on the bed sheets.

E very light went off, dark, dark, dark!

S inister, all alone in the house.

L ips were turning frozen, I was speechless!

E erie silence all around the house.

E verywhere, I could hear whispers, I gasped!

P eering over me, my best friends were telling me to awake.

O nly I was still in bed, it was all a nightmare!

V ery glad it was all a dream.

E veryone's eyes were glued to the window,

R ed blood dripping down!

Tia Desai (11)
Reddiford School, Pinner

A Terrible Nightmare

The waves growled with anger.
With palm trees swaying violently in the breeze.
Monsters crept furtively around me.
There was no time to say *cheese!*

I felt like I was trapped inside,
Their teeth looked like sharp daggers.
Scaly, intimidating scales encompass me,
They were surely worse than a mob of naggers!

A bead of sweat trickled down my forehead
Closer and closer the monsters grew.
Fear stabbed my clammy back,
Go away, horrific monsters, *shoo, shoo, shoo!*

Their talons grate my temples,
Blood was written all over my face.
I wanted to get out of this nightmare,
I desired to run away from this terrible case.

Die, die, die was engraved on the monsters.
My alarm rang with all its might,
I tossed and turned on my bed,
Oh, how this dream gave me a fright!

Shaina Vadher (10)
Reddiford School, Pinner

Once Upon A Magical Dream

Once upon a dream,
I ended up in Candyland.
Transformed into a queen,
With a miniature music band.

Rainbow-coloured unicorns
Soar up in the sky.
Some are munching on Hershey flavoured grass,
Surrounded by chocolate rivers that flow by.

Marshmallow sheep come bounding down the hill,
Just like tumbling cotton balls.
I lay in the nature field, gazing up above,
Making out animals in the fluffy, candyfloss clouds.

I was an athlete, also royalty,
I could fly really high.
I had fairies who would look after me,
Beautiful rainbows in the sky.

The bright sun was nature's queen,
Reigning over her honey-coated kingdom,
Rainbows criss-cross the sky.
At the end of the rainbow was a pot of gold, just for
you and me.

Anya Vidyadhar (9)
Reddiford School, Pinner

The Blood-Sucking Beast

Once I had a bad nightmare,
It was such a frightening scare.
Worse than any evil spiders,
Even worse than bloodsucking vampires.
In fact, it was a made-up creature,
With all the frightening and scary features.

It had fierce, fiery, deathly breath,
Which was sure to give you an instant death.
He chased me with his tentacle feet,
He was catching up, I smelt defeat.

Then it stopped and held its sword high,
It reached all the way up to the sky.
Then, one big slash that hit my head,
I fell in agony - was I dead?

Suddenly, I wake up from my sleep,
The thoughts of the monster in my mind they creep.
But all I have to do is let it go
And dream about something pleasant, like raindrops or
snow.

Aaditya Anant Bhandarkar (10)
Reddiford School, Pinner

The Dark Secret

As I woke up in an abandoned house,
I saw the scattered dust pieces in the gloomy, grey moonlight.
Swiftly swivelling my head around to secure myself,
I saw the shadows where death hid.
The moon gave a wicked grin,
While sending lightning spears and javelins to Earth.
Everything was dead, this must be the Underworld.
I kicked over a pile of skulls and bones,
I wondered if this would be me soon.

That was it - I possibly couldn't take it anymore.
I had to wake up and find a way out.
Running through the twisted, pitch-black corridors until
I hit a dead end,
I flailed my arms around for a torch or a light of some sort.
I found myself staring at a ghost,
Pale and white with deep red, crimson blood,
trickling down its face.

Zahra Elisa Iqbal (10)
Reddiford School, Pinner

Dead Once Asleep

Rocking around in my creaky bed,
My hands turned tense and my black hair crept,
This feeling strangled me and it wouldn't let go,
Holding on to me for a lifelong span.

Gripping onto me, I couldn't escape,
Hiding from it would not make it fake.
Maybe it was my last day awake...

Soon it will go away,
Or maybe it will stay and find its way.
Its jammy legs worked up and down,
Moving slowly to my vast land.

Closer it crept, through nooks and crannies,
Appearing out of nowhere, with its adrenaline eyes.
Blood written all over my face, the death sign
appearing with no wake.
Danger was written in every corner.
Hell had broken free to haunt me all over.

Milen Pattni (10)
Reddiford School, Pinner

Glass House

I wish that I could go back,
but I can only recall
the delicate glasshouse.
Whoa! It was very tall.

With a streaming fountain of shards
and some warm, toasty jars of tarts,
with see-through glass doors
and some mysterious, misty moors.

A hovering, gleaming, glass chandelier
and a shiny crystal bed and furniture.
Logical, leather books with small tears
and a beautiful, clean lounge.

A step...
I look at the amazing world of wonders,
my head is full of thoughts,
I ponder.

I look up and see the Eiffel Tower,
Wow!
I fall flat to the ground.
Bang, bang...
I wake up in my boring bedroom.

Lumanti Bajracharya (11)
Reddiford School, Pinner

Away With The Fairies

I just lost a tooth today,
I was extremely very pleased,
I put it under my pillow,
Then I felt a sneeze.

There was fairy dust all over me,
I think it was the tooth fairy.
My teddy bear, Fluffy, shrank,
Then I turned into a fairy too!

We flew out of the open window
Into the dark street.
Just me, the tooth fairy and Fluffy the bear,
I felt I had to shriek!

Up and up we flew,
Until we reach the moon,
We stopped on a star which was as bright as the sun,
With a hut, very small.

We went inside,
I had a cup of tea.
Then we went back to my house,
I had turned back to me!

Mili Shah (9)
Reddiford School, Pinner

The Dream Of Craziness!

T he dream of good and bad has fairies at every side.
H ere there's crocodiles and alligators and witches
with big eyes.
E vade the magic dust that is sprinkled in the cold air
of the night.

D oom goes boom, then bang, destroying your sight!
R ight when one tree grows up and one tree goes
down.
E xpect a screaming pig, dressed up like a clown
A nd at midnight in Dreamland, my sweat has
increased.
M y heart, pale, stopping when I see some sharp teeth.

I open my eyes.

H eading to the fridge
A nd realised again that my
D ream hadn't finished!

Vernilan Vishnukumar (11)
Reddiford School, Pinner

What's My Dream Palace?

When I open the doors to my dreams,
I look at the things which are important to me.
I look at my bed, encrusted with diamonds on the side,
Then my roof, which has a golden chandelier.
Also, in my dream I have no fear.

Next, I go into my garden,
It really makes me feel small.
I cannot even see my back wall.
It is infinite, that's all I can say
And I think what lies at the end of it day by day.

I think now, I've shown you my home
And you have seen the power of dreams.
They teleport you into a magical land.
You might meet a lava man,
But you remember whatever you want is whatever you dream.

Furqan Qadir
Reddiford School, Pinner

Unicorn

Big, soft and cute unicorns flying around like fairies
casting spells.
Candyfloss trees as fluffy as a cloud,
soft, milky, chocolate grass.

Houses made from gingerbread, ice cream slides that
take you up and down.
Chocolate chip cookie windows, chocolate sofas,
that can be as big as you'd like them to be.

Cola water slides, that take you into cola pools,
too many rooms to count,
jelly bed, cupcake-shaped houses and a jelly force field.

Whoosh! It's a lollipop aeroplane.
Bang! There are ice cream fireworks.
I see toffee shops with a candy cane playground.

Alveena Dudhia (8)
Reddiford School, Pinner

Evil Clowns

E verywhere are the evil clowns waiting for someone to pass by.

V ery sneaky are the clowns, they hide in bushes and wait for you.

I ntelligent but scary, they wait until you are close to jump out and scare you.

L ight is not an option, they only come out when night's as black as coal.

C unning, with big, curly hair.

L iving through battles and through fights.

O ozing blood left on the floor.

W etting the floor with all the water that they drink.

N ever-ending fun for them.

S cary as thunder and lightning booming down on the Earth.

James Gibbs
Reddiford School, Pinner

Dreamy Dream

Shooting stars going by, while my eyes are closed.
Sleep to dream, dream to sleep,
I have not yet decided.
Dreaming of having a chocolate factory or becoming a
journalist.

Having a chocolate factory like Willy Wonka,
Slurping on delicious, fancy chocolate and toffee.
The factory workers made of hard chocolate,
Chocolate melting after a few hours.

Dancing with silly clowns,
Clowns making poses.
Clowns with multicoloured noses,
Finally, they reached down.

Having a pet fairy,
Helping me get my dictionary.
They are not even scary,
Not even wary.

Anushka Srisuthan
Reddiford School, Pinner

One Day

It was as beautiful
as a majestic butterfly.
The next door's gingerbread man
was using his chocolate milk
to water his chocolate tree.

Until...
Crash,
Bang!

A vegetable monster
shot his bright, corn bullet
at the gingerbread man's window.

Then pulled his carrot sword
and cut the sweet air in half.
Then it flew into the sky
and cooked him with his fiery eyes.

But then, I saw ahead,
the destruction of Sweet City
by an army of vegetable monsters.

All of a sudden I woke up!

Matthew Dancer (8)
Reddiford School, Pinner

Nightmares

M y heart is beating like a billion drums
Y ew trees are stopping my escape

N ight-time, the deadliest time in the day
I n my head, I'm telling myself to keep running
G ot to get back home, away from the monster
H ot and sweaty, I'm struggling to keep it up
T ired and weary, I'm facing my fear
M y scariest nightmare is what this is
A ll alone in the dark wood, in my mind
R ealising slowly, that it's alright, it's just a nightmare
E ntering a good dream now, everything is safe and
fine

Anusha Choubina (11)
Reddiford School, Pinner

Last Night In My Crazy Dream

Last night, in my crazy dream,
I had superpowers.
How amazing!
I even teleported into fairy towers.

Last night, in my crazy dream,
I had freeze-breath.
So very cold,
Well, that's what I have been told.

Last night, in my crazy dream,
I had laser eyes.
I was very hungry,
So I heated up some pies.

Last night, in my crazy dream,
I teleported.
So very strange,
I was reported.

Last night, in my crazy dreams,
I had telekinesis,
I couldn't control,
It was a phenomenon.

Tomisin Esther Shitta-Bey (10)
Reddiford School, Pinner

A Dream

I find myself playing on some green leaves
I run away who knows if I will be
seen again.
I see a stone wall in front of me
I run across the fragile drawbridge
which snaps in half by the time I'm over.
The sparkling moat
the crumbly ground beneath
me rises and throws me at tree.
I hit with impact, the tree
is broken.
I run to another tree.
A cloud falls before me in the shape of a sofa
I sit down and rest.
There is only relaxation, no dehydration.
Now I get up
in the real world.
For now, my dream is over.

Joshua Griffith (8)
Reddiford School, Pinner

The Best Singer Ever!

What I want to be is very easy.
What I want to be is very dreamy.
Open your eyes, you're in for a surprise,
because I want to be a singer!
The microphones call to me as I walk past,
shining like diamonds, the stage pulls me in.
I'll sing all day,
I'll sing all night,
I'll be on X Factor all right!
I'll be a solo singer
and I will rock the stage every night.
The crowd will go wild and I'm telling you, I'm right.
This is my dream.
I'll have some fun.
Tell the world
I'll be the one.

Anjali Kylahsum (9)
Reddiford School, Pinner

Summer Dream

It was a hot summer's day
the sky could never be grey,
it was like no tomorrow,
no one could ever feel sorrow.

The wind was singing, the trees were dancing,
it was so much fun and everyone was laughing,
with the lemonade in hand
and a very bouncy party band.

With my friends by my side
let us enjoy this ride.
As I dance all about
whilst we sing and we shout.

My heart keeps pumping
and my feet keep thumping.
As I roam around in my head
and am tucked away in my sweet bed.

Swastha Shankar (11)
Redditord School, Pinner

Once Upon A Dream

In my bed,
I felt like I flew in the sky.
When I woke up, I was sitting on a transport ship
looking through the clouds.
Seeing lots of planets, like Jupiter and Pluto.
I touched some to see how they were,
soft, like a comfortable cushion
on a shining star in the middle of space.
Mercury, cold like snow.
Mars, as hot as molten lava.
All of the planets were moving slowly
right next to each other.
Everything was beautiful,
as colourful as a rainbow.
Finally, I was back in my bed.
Please, dream, come back.

Dylan Kankeyan Devabala (9)
Reddiford School, Pinner

My Strange Dream

Am I awake or am I asleep?
The fairies are my best friends.
Will this strange dream ever end?
My pet dragon is what I am riding,
All the unicorns come out of hiding.
The mole did a forward roll,
Straight into his odd hole!
I saw the sun heat up the beach,
While the seagulls screech, keeping out of reach.
I saw the funny dolphin grin,
As he waggled his spotty, pink fin.
Then I heard the strangest thing;
Ding-a ling-a-ling-a-ling.
I woke to the sound of the shrill alarm,
It was a dream all along!

Rihanna Radia (11)
Reddiford School, Pinner

Dream Land

In Dream Land the sun is always shining
no thunderstorms ever, or
the Mayor of Peace will be coming.
You can hear the birds chirping
from very far away
and the giants are burping
two thousand times a day.
Lying in bed, or going to Dream Land.
In Dream Land
if you work as mayor
you only get one pound.
The clouds taste like cotton candy
and the trees look like broccoli.
My favourite game in Dream Land
is World Map Monopoly.
When you're in Dream Land
your worries are gone.

Karina Desai (8)
Reddiford School, Pinner

Nightmares

N ow I'm in a place I've never seen,
I n a place I've never been.
G oing into a dream.
H aunted by this horrible feeling.
T his situation should be sealing.
M y body senses something coming, it's going to be here in a while.
A ppearing in sight; I see its beckoning smile.
R aging with fiery anger, it said,
'E ventually I will kill you straight, you'll be dead.'
S uddenly I woke up to find, I'm home in bed!

Roshan Arora
Reddiford School, Pinner

Candyland

Reading my book slowly puts me to bed,
Then I said,
'What a good idea to step into the book,
Let me go into Candyland and have a little look.'

As I enter,
I find myself in the centre.
Did I really fly
or is this just a lie?

On the ground is marshmallow grass
And I also passed
A milk chocolate waterfall which I desire,
Also white chocolate trees which I admire.

As I go back to my bed I said,
'Goodness sake,
is this fake?'

Shreya Ashish Patel (10)
Reddiford School, Pinner

Monsters Of The Night

I go to sleep and I wake up.
Wait, this is not where I left off.
I arise, startled,
Sweat running down my face.
What is this devil's place?
Ghost hovering, wail!
I see everything, yet everything is shrouded.
The walls closing,
The roof creaks.
I stare at crimson blood, it trickles down my face.
Where am I?
The pale vampire bares its teeth,
Ready to strike.
I stare death in the face,
No! I wake with a jolt,
My mind is swirling,
I've been to Hell!

Avi Juneja (10)
Reddiford School, Pinner

Candyland

I jump into Candyland,
Which is all upside down.
I try to walk in the chocolatey sand,
But it's really brown!

I realise, I'm standing on my head,
I get back on my fabulous feet
Which were buried in the sand
As still as a pencil lead!

I glance at the candyfloss-covered house,
With tiramisu doors,
I wish I could eat the mouse
Running around on the rocky road floors.

Unfortunately, I jolt awake,
Still trying to attempt to bake.

Amey Gupta (10)
Reddiford School, Pinner

Nightmares?

Nightmares peeping in my bed,
Why do these nightmares have to come into my head?
Will these nightmares come alive?
I don't think I can survive!
Running quickly to capture me,
I'm begging you, let me free!
Giving me such a fright,
Not letting me go to bed at night.

They do not obey
And they make the dreams go away.
They always make a creepy sound
Whenever they are around.
Trying not to sleep in the day,
Does this have to be the way?

Harini Thirupaharan (10)
Reddiford School, Pinner

Dream Land

Candyfloss trees dancing in the wind.
A chocolate river flowing like the sea.
I look at the sky and the sun gives me a smile.
Dream Land! I'm really in Dream Land.

Mammoth, fluffy, white clouds exactly like pillows.
Pink-haired unicorns run around on the green grass of
fields.

House made out of chips with an ice cream roof.
White chocolate as wallpaper with doughnut windows.
Mouth-watering, veggie burger door.

Georgia Moore (8)
Reddiford School, Pinner

All Night, No Sleep

Last night I had a dream,
now my mind is clean.
Trying to go to sleep,
something I can't keep.

I wish I could dream,
lying in the moonbeams,
I can't seem to keep still,
keep on fidgeting, until...

Starting to fall asleep
then something began to be.
It was my alarm clock,
tossing over to turn it off.

I just want to go to sleep.
Why won't it work for me?

Ashna Jitesh Halai
Reddiford School, Pinner

Dragon's Dream

It was warm under my covers,
as I snuggled in my bed.
All of a sudden
I entered Dreamland.
Cold now, I felt the breeze,
my body began to tremble,
shaking, but not because of the temperature...
A massive dragon appeared, flying through the sky,
fire spewing out of its mouth,
burning down my house.
Now I was frightened
and grabbed a golden sword,
slayed the dragon easily,
it died like a lord.

Shayam Jayesh Patel (9)
Reddiford School, Pinner

A Winter Wonderland

I close my eyes and think and find myself in a winter wonderland.
The snowflakes falling every step you go, *pitter-patter.*
Winter animals staying in their nest.
It smells like fresh snow.
All trees have flowers that are blue and green
Everything looks like iced cupcakes.
All lakes are frozen with ice.
It may be cold, but it is warm inside.
Once you've been, you never want to leave.

Harshita Sinha (9)
Reddiford School, Pinner

Gymnasts

The roaring crowd of fans
clapping with their hands
waiting for the girls
to do their graceful twirls.

With my great team
walking carefully on the beam.
Scared as can be
till we fall free.

We are the best
finished our great quest.
We have one
now we can have fun.

We may just win next time
if we do it will be fine.

Tiya Roma Patel (9)
Reddiford School, Pinner

Dreams

Dreams are like a cloud striding across the sky,
Sometimes they wave to me.
They look like they are going to reach to the sky.
In my bed,
At dawn,
I wonder how I see these extraordinary things.
Then, I start to fall asleep in my cosy bed,
Then I see the most strange thing.
Thousands of clowns standing together,
All with a disapproving frown.
Dreams are fun.

Arnav Dubey
Reddiford School, Pinner

Gameland Adventure!

I'm with my favourite
game character, he is as
fast as a cheetah,
his house is a stadium.

To open the door he has a
secret code, instead of stairs
he has a trampoline,
he has competitions against his friends.

I play against him, but
smack, *bang*, he
beats me every time.
I try my best,
but I lose and lose.

Krish Naik (8)
Reddiford School, Pinner

Dream World

Once I had a dream,
That wasn't quite me,
I had been teleported to a world
Where all was strange.

Candy canes were walking,
Flowers were talking,
Clouds were fighting,
But the sun was illuminating.

I walked in a trance,
To the end of the path.
Oh, how this strange dream world
made me laugh.

Anay Vaghela-Shah (10)
Reddiford School, Pinner

Dream Or Nightmare?

Twisting and turning in my bed
Finally, falling off
My brain took me to a haunted house
The cracked walls look damp
Roofs with bats on them
I entered the gloomy house
Millions of statues caught my eye
Whenever I moved, the statues moved closer and
closer
I could hear it
I want this dream to stop.
Eyes wide open...

Dilan Amin (9)
Reddiford School, Pinner

Let's Get Whacking!

I once had a dream about a cricketer,
his name was Pradyun Sushena.
He hit all balls
four sixes and fours
and he gave out his signature.

One day he was versus Beijing,
he said, 'Let's get whacking!'
He went too big
and his time was up, *ding!*
He said, 'Why am I departing?'

Pradyun Sushena (9)
Reddiford School, Pinner

Once I Went To A Fancy Forest

Once I went to a fancy forest
but instead, I got lost
it was getting dark.

The trees started to turn into swamp monsters,
they smelt like rotten cheese.

My heart raced,
I was scared and alone.
How I wished my mum was here.

All of a sudden,
I found myself cosy in my room.

Samuel Rao Yarasani
Reddiford School, Pinner

Eat A Rainbow

I would like to be a king
And rule the world.
I would like to live in a house
With a golden interior and walls made out of ice cream
As big as a mansion.
Time to time, the house would float on the soft, white
clouds.
I would like to eat ice cream sundaes every day,
Be a millionaire
And finally, eat a rainbow.

Syun Patel
Reddiford School, Pinner

The Alien

In the endless vacuum of space, it floats around
In a saucer, it comes to Earth to abduct our hopeless kind.
Toxins linger in its moist, green skin
Its angry, red eyes, like a nightmare they pull you into your fate.
It lurks around in the depths of my head,
But don't let it escape...
The alien.

Dylan Patel
Reddiford School, Pinner

Death Of The Wizards

In my dreams I dreamt about wizards
and as he gave his spell - lizards.
As I tried to fight him,
he changed to a little thing.
Finally, I slashed my sword,
he just said what I wanted,
that, 'I was his Lord.'
As he died in pain,
I knew his little game,
that he just wanted peace.

Ravi Karan Shah
Reddiford School, Pinner

Dream On

I fall asleep in my comfy bed,
When I wake up, I realise I'm in the sky.
I look down, I start to panic
I'm floating like a balloon.
Ice cream starts to fall
From the big, blue, twinkly sky.
When it's time to wake up
I don't want to
But I know I can dream again tomorrow.

Kareena Ahluwalia (9)
Reddiford School, Pinner

The Amazing Fashion Designer!

What I want to be is a famous fashion designer.
I'm all alone, trying to think what to design next.
I see a little girl walking past my studio
With candyfloss in her hand.
An extraordinary idea struck me,
I was going to make a candyfloss jumpsuit.

This is what my dream is!

Ashvika Kotha
Reddiford School, Pinner

Dragons

Once I had a dragon's dream,
there was this fire-breathing dragon,
who had teeth shaped like grey daggers
and a long green tail, shaped like an ice cream cone.
Unfortunately, it had large yellow wings,
it also had sharp claws attached to its flappy wings.
Once I had a dream.

Rohan Parmar (10)
Reddiford School, Pinner

I Am A Dragon

I am a dragon.
I whoosh up into the air.
After a few minutes
Everyone stares.
I glide to the clouds,
Peer down and see crowds.
I breathe my fire,
Causing confusion and fear.
But now my dream is ended,
I am not a dragon,
Just an ordinary boy.

Zak Kupfer (9)
Reddiford School, Pinner

The Galaxy

The galaxy is as beautiful as a snow globe
As I look for peace and quiet.
The moon tastes like cotton candy.
As I sit on the earth
It feels so soft,
It feels as if I am holding a golden moon.
Mars feels peppery,
As if it's a volcano.

Boluwatife Anidugbe (8)
Reddiford School, Pinner

As I Shut My Eyes

As I shut my eyes I got indulged in a world of darkness.
A world where I was completely powerless.

My bed became a blanket of thorns
And there and then my nightmare was born.

Trees arched and towered above me.
And in my head I wondered... would I ever be free?

Then I saw it, saw him, saw the man.
As soon as I saw him I staggered up and ran.

I ran and ran as fast as I could.
Through the old, haunted wood.

Greta Pitts (11)
Slinfold CE Primary School, Slinfold

The 5th Of November

My dreams can take me anywhere,
Through the wind or in the sky,
Or with the sea whilst singing a lullaby,
I would dream any day.

To a haunted mansion,
Which is full of the dead,
I still sleep,
In my bed.

With shivering bones,
And caveman moans,
I would dream,
Any day.

To the Land of Sweets,
And sick old beats,
Where the DJs rule,
And there ain't no school.

With shivering bones,
And caveman moans,
I would dream,
Any day.

To the Land of Animals,
Where there ain't no cannibals,
But without no sleep,
People just want a jeep.

With shivering bones,
And caveman moans,
I would dream,
Any day.

But when I wake up,
I realise that it's just a dream,
But I will still remember,
The 5th of November.

The night when all was true!

Ryan McWatt (11)
Slinfold CE Primary School, Slinfold

To The World To Come

To the world to come
I will sing a song to the new world tomorrow
A song of love and laughter
A new world of peace and love
A new world when nations will love nations,
When there will be no war.
When children won't lose their parents and loved ones.
When children won't suffer for the mistakes of others.
When children won't be denied the power of education.

I will sing a song to the new world to come
A song of freedom for all
A song of how beautiful the world would be if we live at
peace with all.
A song of no killing and fighting
A song of love over hate
A song of waking up from my dream when everyone
would smile at each other when they meet.

When we can share the little we have with those in
need.
When we can reach out to help.

I will sing a song to the new world to come.
The world I see in my dreams
A world beautiful to live in.

A world that will make each and everyone have respect for one another
A world that will be united forever,
This is my dream.
To wake up and sing this song to the new world to come.

Brian Delali Tsikata (8)
St Philip's Catholic Primary School, Arundel

Magnificent Munching Mantis

P lant tendrils wrapped around my burning leg
R ed flowers dripped nectar onto me and the mantis
A ll of a sudden, the mantis shuddered and grew
Y es! I shouted as I clung onto his giant leg
I n a flash I was among the treetops
N early knocked a monkey off his branch!
G rabbed a branch and swung away.

M antis turned as red as flames
A s the skies turned black as ink
N ow with eyes shining like a mirror
T rampled after me like a giant
I woke up panting and staring
S uddenly, my mantis stared back!

Claude Young (8)
St Philip's Catholic Primary School, Arundel

Ballerina

B allerina is elegant and quiet as night
A utumn leaves as red as a fox, change is coming
L aughing and dancing
L eaves full of magic
E lves and unicorns and fairies dancing through the night
R eady for the change of season
I n and out of trees, dancers between the leaves
N ow all is silent for the fairy has gone
A ll is quiet and calm.

Autumn Sleven (7)
St Philip's Catholic Primary School, Arundel

Candyland

Wow! This is amazing,
so many sweets and chocolate,
unicorns, a shiny sun
and a rainbow river.

I never knew this existed,
this is almost like Heaven.
Oh and look at the chocolate fountain,
I want to have a shower in that.

I can see three people over there,
from here they do look familiar,
they look very friendly too,
'Hello! Oh, it's you!'

It was Mrs Campbell, (my very joyful teacher)
There were two other people too,
Aaliyah and Phoebe, they were my school friends.

That time I knew
I going to have so much fun
and what I thought
was completely true!

We played Candy Catch (a very popular game in
Candyland)
with Mr Unicorn, (who was an actual moving unicorn),
until we were so tired, that we
couldn't get off the comfortable, on the candy cushion.

Suddenly Aaliyah disappeared
and then so did Phoebe and then Mrs Campbell
and then suddenly me.
So that was the end of my dream.

Ammarah Ahmed (10)
Yeading Junior School, Hayes

Daring Dreams

You can be the author who writes the amazing books,
or be the stylist who gives the designer looks.
Maybe you want to be a waitress, who serves all the
special dishes,
perhaps you want to be a fisherman, who catches all
the fishes.

Daring dreams,
devious schemes.

You can be a doctor, who cures all their patients that
are ill,
or be a chef in a restaurant, who can whip up a grill.
Maybe you might be a postman, who delivers all the
mail,
as well as being a police officer, who takes criminals to
jail.

Daring dreams,
devious schemes.

Your salary may be high or low,
hard work could make it grow.
Go on! Because you have something to show,
find the treasure near the rainbow.

Dionne Pylypets Rabi (10)
Yeading Junior School, Hayes

Wonder Land

Whenever I feel distant
or when I can't concentrate
when my head is spinning, spinning
when I can't resist

I would even refuse
the friendliest of hands
who've got the joyful news.
He will whisk me away to Wonderland.

All my thoughts go whizzing
books, pens and the BFP,
(he's the Big Friendly Poet you see)
Wonderland, the place when you need to fantasise.

This is why I never, ever refuse
the friendliest of hands,
who's got the joyful news,
will whisk me away to Wonderland.

Just when I'm settling
someone has to ruin it all,
because the nightmare really starts
when I've snapped out of my daydreams.

Alia Ali
Yeading Junior School, Hayes

Fear Of Death

As I walked past the trees
I tried to get past the leaves.
I shivered with ease
I opened the door
There was a knife in front of me.

I tried to get under
I heard the sound of thunder.
Next thing I saw
Was dead bugs on the floor.

I got past the knives
Next thing I saw were ghosts.
It was like having anxiety stop
I walked through the ghost
Next thing I heard loud screams.

Then, I felt like someone was following me
There were cracked and shattered windows.
There was a solid door
I walked up to the door.

The door was locked.
I tried and tried to open the door.
I hear sounds of footsteps
Then the door opened...

Leo Ojara (10)
Yeading Junior School, Hayes

The Dream I Could Never Forget

Detention, detention, detention.
I could see my reflection in a mirror which was facing me.
My hands reached to the mirror,
I was sucked into the mirror and transported
to a land with rainbows, candy and unicorns.

It must have been a secret
that Mrs Campbell was hiding.
she was marking with candy in her mouth,
was jamming out to music and dancing with unicorns.

We had to find our way back, I couldn't stay there.
The portal, where was it?
Mrs Campbell, Mrs Campbell, Mrs Campbell, what are we going to do?

What, Mrs Goddard! What was she doing there?
She was next to the portal,
my heart pounded as I woke up,
it was a dream.

Tanisha Kaur (10)
Yeading Junior School, Hayes

The Consequences Of Unkindness

There were once evil fairies
who wanted to destroy the town.
They tried to be scary
but they always wore a frown.

Later on, Mrs Campbell was caught,
she turned bad.
We were all distraught,
everyone mad.

Mrs Campbell is a witch,
do not dare to snitch
for, within a twitch
you will be an ostrich.

Mrs Goddard, are you nice?
Please give me some advice.
make Mrs Campbell polite,
ensuring the evil fairies life is bright.

Mrs Goddard was kind,
Mrs Campbell was fined.
But she was still mean,
so they turned her into a bean.

Roble Warsame (10)
Yeading Junior School, Hayes

Neptune's Fame

Space, space such a wonderful place
while the sun gazes at me
I wonder what lies behind the moon.
Maybe rocks, maybe stars, who knows?
But suddenly, I find myself floating
I hadn't noticed the smile
shining on Neptune!
It's big googly eyes blinking at me
I zoom towards the planet
wondering how magical it might be.
Its colour was as bright as a rainbow
but suddenly
I could not see
the planet right in front of me!
'Time for school,' said Mum.
It was just a dream!

Eliora Efrem (10)
Yeading Junior School, Hayes

Mrs Unicorn

Mrs Unicorn please come back
I really want to see you.
I've got everything I need, already packed
But how do I get to you?
Mrs Unicorn, please come back
I really miss your shimmering horn.
I could never sleep
Even though I yawn.
Mrs Unicorn, please come back
I love your rainbow tail
It's so shiny
And I didn't know you had glittering nails.
Mrs Unicorn, oh, please come back
How can I ever live without you?

Harmanpreet Chahal (10)
Yeading Junior School, Hayes

Shiver Me Timbers

I went to bed
and I saw a pirate ship,
I met Jack Sparrow
who was cleaning the barrels.
Then I met Will Turner,
who was admiring the sparrows.

I climbed the ropes to see where I was,
then the water shook,
then I fell into the sea.
I swam and I swam, but then
came out of the blue,
a monster who ate me.
I woke up.

Satwinder Kaur Sandhu (10)
Yeading Junior School, Hayes

The Queen Needs My Help!

I was in an unknown place
and then the Queen arrived.
I was in a sort of base
but then I noticed, I was
in the Queen's hideout.
She needed my help
to destroy an evil wizard.
What should I do?
Should I help the Queen
or not?
At that moment I could
not decide, because
I woke up.

Layane Ali (9)
Yeading Junior School, Hayes

The Treasure Island

I was on an unknown island
I spotted some figures walking towards me
I notice they were pirates
and I saw a magnificent ship sitting in the sea.
I was on Treasure Island
there was treasure around me and a genie.
I was stuck
I hope the genie gives luck.

Vaughan Kirubakar (10)
Yeading Junior School, Hayes

Est.1991

YOUNG WRITERS INFORMATION

We hope you have enjoyed reading this book – and that you will continue to in the coming years.

If you're a young writer who enjoys reading and creative writing, or the parent of an enthusiastic poet or story writer, do visit our website **www.youngwriters.co.uk**. Here you will find free competitions, workshops and games, as well as recommended reads, a poetry glossary and our blog.

If you would like to order further copies of this book, or any of our other titles, then please give us a call or visit **www.youngwriters.co.uk**.

Young Writers
Remus House
Coltsfoot Drive
Peterborough
PE2 9BF
(01733) 890066
info@youngwriters.co.uk